Irredentism and
International Politics

Studies in International Politics

*The Leonard Davis Institute
for International Relations,
The Hebrew University of Jerusalem*

A volume in the series
Adamantine International Studies

Published in the United States of America in 1991 by
Lynne Rienner Publishers, Inc.
1800 30th Street, Boulder, Colorado 80301

and in the United Kingdom by
Adamantine Press Limited
419 Richmond Road, Twickenham TW1 2EX

Library of Congress Cataloging-in-Publication Data
Chazan, Naomi, 1946–
    Irredentism and international politics / by Naomi Chazan.
        p.   cm.
    Includes bibliographical references (p.   ) and index.
    ISBN 1-55587-221-2
    1. Irredentism. 2. International relations. 3. Boundaries.
4. Territory, National. 5. Ethnic groups. 6. World politics.
I. Title.
JX4088.C43 1990   90-9010
341.4'2––dc20   CIP

British Cataloguing in Publication Data
Irredentism and international politics.—(Adamantine International Studies;
ISSN 0954—607 3: no. 7)
1. Territorial claims. Disputes, history
I. Chazan, Naomi, *1946–*
341.42
ISBN 0-7449-0033-6

The maps in Chapter 4 are derived from maps published in *Andrees Hand Atlas Siebente Auflage* (Bielefeld and Leipzig: Verlag von Velhagen & Klasing, 1921).

Printed and bound in the United States of America

The paper used in this publication meets the requirements
of the American National Standard for Permanence of
Paper for Printed Library Materials Z39.48-1984.

Irredentism and International Politics

◆

edited by
Naomi Chazan

Lynne Rienner Publishers ◆ Boulder
Adamantine Press Limited ◆ London

Contents

Maps

Acknowledgments _____

Most of the contributions to this book were first presented at a workshop held at the Center for International Studies at the Massachusetts Institute of Technology in April 1986, under the sponsorship of the Leonard Davis Institute of International Relations of the Hebrew University of Jerusalem. The participation of Walker Connor, Dov Ronen, Timothy Shaw, and Myron Weiner was critical in conceptualizing the study and in supplying guidelines for the thorough revision of the chapters. Gabriel Sheffer, codirector of the Leonard Davis Institute, has been the moving spirit behind the project, which is part of a larger study of trans-state ethnic and religious networks and their influence on international politics. David Hornik, Judith Fattal, and Anna Thee provided crucial editorial and administrative assistance, and deserve special thanks for bringing this volume to completion.

Irredentism and
International Politics

Approaches to the Study of Irredentism

NAOMI CHAZAN

Ethnicity has reemerged as a major issue in international politics. In the last decade of the twentieth century, the breakdown of the Soviet bloc on the one hand and the attempt at West European consolidation and German reunification on the other have highlighted the tenuous connection between state boundaries and historical, cultural, and symbolic communities. One aspect of the international politics of ethnicity focuses on the demarcation of state frontiers; a second is concerned with the role of diaspora communities in global affairs;[1] a third centers on irredentism, a phenomenon highlighted by the Iraqi invasion of Kuwait in August 1990.

Irredentism is an outgrowth of the complexities inherent in the notion of the nation-state. The state, a legal-territorial concept, refers to that set of structures and institutions that seek to maintain effective control over a given population within a specifically defined geographical area. The nation relates to the psychocultural phenomenon of a group of people possessing a common symbolic referent and joint aspirations and who desire to give political expression to these identities.[2] The term nation-state has come into use to denote those states in which national and political frontiers coincide.

In most instances, the boundaries of existing states do not precisely coincide with those of groups who perceive themselves as culturally cohesive units and wish to demonstrate their solidarity politically. In these cases, the quest of ethnic groups for self-determination has given rise to separatist movements whose demands range from autonomy to full independence, as well as to irredentist claims by governments that seek to retrieve ethnic kin and their territories from neighboring states.[3]

Irredentism, therefore, is distinct from, but closely related to, separatism.[4] The term irredentism (derived from the Italian *irredenta*—unredeemed) was first used to refer to the Italian movement to annex Italian-speaking areas under Austrian and Swiss rule during the nineteenth century. It has since come to encompass any political effort to unite ethnically, historically, or geographically related segments of a population in adjacent countries within a common political framework.

The purpose of this book is to shed light on the key facets of

1

irredentism in historical and comparative perspective. The contributors examine the determinants, the dynamics, and the consequences of irredentism as it affects the policies of countries and groups making irredentist claims and of those against whom claims are being made. Given the renewed interest in the redefinition of state boundaries, a particular emphasis is placed on the external dimensions of these processes.

PROBLEMS OF ANALYSIS

Definition

Irredentism, with its emphasis on the political unification of self-conscious communities, highlights the importance of people and the land they occupy in the determination of the frontiers of the state. Two major types of irredentist claims are recognized in the literature. The first, and by far the most prominent, is a situation in which a certain ethnic group is a majority in the state making irredentist claims and a minority in a neighboring country. Irredentism in this situation refers to the demand made by a government to incorporate its conationalists and the territory they occupy across the border into the parent state, and/or to the demands made by the people involved that they be reunited with their kin across the border. This type of irredentist claim includes, historically, the Greeks in Albania and Turkey, the Germans in Czechoslovakia and Poland, and the Croats in Austria and Yugoslavia. Contemporary cases abound: the Somalis in Ethiopia, the Muslims in Kashmir, the Swazis in the Republic of South Africa, or the Ewe in Ghana. It does not, however, refer to the efforts to reunite the two Germanies, Chinas, or Koreas, where political differences separate groups that view themselves as culturally or historically cohesive.

The second and far more ambiguous type of irredentist claim is one in which the ethnic group is a minority in two or more countries: the Slovenians in Austria and Yugoslavia; the Macedonians in Bulgaria, Yugoslavia, and Greece; the Pushtans in Afghanistan and Pakistan; the Armenians in the Soviet Union, Turkey, and Iran; the Tajiks and Uzbeks in the Soviet Union and Afghanistan; the Azerbayjanis in the Soviet Union and Iran; and the Kurds in Turkey, Iran, and Iraq. In such cases, the ethnic group may seek union with one of the countries, or it may call for independent statehood (and, indeed, the group is frequently divided internally precisely on this question). A variant of this second type may be a situation in which components of multiethnic states have irredentist claims aimed at creating entirely new nation-states. The Kurdish demand for statehood falls directly into this category, as does the Armenian example. In both these instances, however, there is no parent state to press ethnic claims, and hence there is uncertainty regarding the classification of these cases.[5]

Thus, although it is clear that not every border dispute is irredentist, the matter of recognition and identification of irredenta is not as clear cut as it might appear on the surface. One would not suggest that the Argentinian claim on the Falklands was irredentist because the islands do not contain an Argentinian population. Similarly, the boundary disputes between China and India and between China and the Soviet Union may hardly be defined as irredentist because the relationships between land and people play such minor roles in these conflicts.

One would, however, characterize Afghanistan's demand for the incorporation of the Pushtu-speaking areas of Pakistan as irredentist. So, too, is Pakistan's claim on Indian Kashmir on the ground that its population is Muslim. The historical demands of Germany on sections of Poland, of Greece on Turkey and Bulgaria, of Iraq on Kuwait, and of Bulgaria on the Macedonian region of Yugoslavia also fall fairly neatly into an irredentist mold.

But between these extremes lie certain cases, such as the Palestinian one, which may not be irredentist at certain historical points, but under other circumstances might be deemed to be of an irredentist nature. The Palestinian demand for a state in the West Bank and Gaza is not irredentist, but rather one for statehood. But a Jordanian demand for the return of these territories to Jordan might have an irredentist component, as would a claim by a future Palestinian state for parts of Jerusalem or for the absorption of the Arab-populated areas of Israel. Similarly, an Israeli claim to sovereignty over Greater Israel has irredentist overtones.

The definition of irredentism therefore requires refinement and elaboration, with particular emphasis on the possible fluidity of irredentism in specific historical and situational contexts. Concentrating on clear-cut case studies, this book attempts to sharpen current definitions of irredentist phenomena and to demarcate their outstanding features.

Variables

The contributors to this book are concerned with explaining irredentism and how it affects relations between states. Irredentism encompasses two major variables: states and ethnic, cultural, historical, and/or geographically defined groups. Each of these might wish to maintain or alter the status quo. Depending on the degree to which they are willing to pursue the objective of political change, the prospects for the intensification or repression of irredentism vary and so, too, do the types of interstate conflict and possible solutions.

The form and composition of each of these components is therefore significant. Putative irredentist states may be monoethnic in makeup, or they may be states in which one group forms a clear majority. Alternately, irredentist demands may be pressed by multiethnic states, especially if the political position of claimant groups is particularly strong. Similarly, the delineation of the collectivity to be redeemed may vary. Ethnicity surely defines many groups that are the object of irredentist takeovers. But these groups may also be defined by religion, historical affinity, language, or geography. The nature of the state with irredentist dispositions and of the groups and territories involved may affect the dynamics of irredentism in important ways.

A multiplicity of factors thus comes into play in the analysis of the complex interaction of loyalties and claims made by states and transborder peoples. These include structural considerations, such as the relative power of competing states; the existence of common institutions among the divided societies; the size, concentration, and dispersal of the people involved; the degree of intragroup communication; and the porousness of borders. Normative concerns are also important: the salience of various symbolic referents, ideological factors, and the degree of group identification. The precise role of economic variables (access to resources, economic opportunities on both sides of the border, economic prospects); social components (existing modes of stratification, levels of literacy, degree of urbanization, patterns of individual and group mobility, prevalence of social conflict); policy issues (the ethnic policy of different states, cultural and economic orientations, political preferences, expansionist tendencies); historical preconditions (the preexistence of common political institutions, political history, social and economic changes, past record of conflict or coexistence); and, of course, intrastate and global variables must be delineated.

By identifying the most significant factors affecting states and ethnic groups at each phase of the irredentist process, the contributors attempt to lay the foundation for a more comprehensive understanding of this facet of trans-state ethnic and cultural relations.

Issues

Irredentism is a dynamic process; its analysis requires coming to grips with certain fundamental questions that in turn require detailed investigation and comparison. The chapters in this book address several core questions related to this dynamic.

The first issue concerns the conditions under which irredentist claims are made. Is there a connection between the political position of the divided people and their quest for reunification? Can the circumstances for the rise of irredentism be tied to specific policies, resources, economic opportunities, global conditions, or social and political institutions of the state making irredentist demands? What is the role of levels of literacy, or even the size and concentration of specific groups and their degree of interaction in the rise of irredentism?

A closer analysis of the particular constellation of factors that can account for the presentation of irredentist claims can help to illuminate not only the framework within which specific irredentist processes have taken place, but also why in many instances irredentist tendencies have been circumscribed. Africa is a continent replete with examples of ethnic groups divided by international boundaries (the Yoruba in Nigeria and Benin; the Berbers in Algeria, Tunisia, and Libya; the Tutsi in Rwanda and Burundi; the Afars in Djibouti and Ethiopia; the Khoi-Khoisan in Botswana and Namibia; the Hausa in Nigeria, Niger, and Ghana; the Akan in Ghana and Côte d'Ivoire; the Bakongo in Angola and Zaire; and many more). But given the ubiquity of ethnic separation on the African continent, the number of irredentist movements has been markedly low. Similarly, Switzerland and Malaysia have not evinced irredentist tendencies, whereas many of their neighbors have been engaged in such conflicts for years. Some of the reasons for quiescence in these areas may be gleaned from a comparison with the conditions that have nurtured irredentism elsewhere.

A second issue centers on who raises the irredentist demands: is it the government of the majority state, a group within that state, the minority group that wishes to reunite with the state where cohorts have a majority, or several minorities in concert? The organization of the irredentist movement, its social composition, its leadership, and its internal structure are of some importance in comprehending both the intensity and the scope of specific instances of irredentism. Answers to these questions may also help to identify the precise starting point of irredentist processes, and thus also assist in accounting for the effects of irredentist claims on each of the parties, their relations with each other, and their foreign alliances.

A third dimension of the irredentist dynamic involves the nature of the irredentist demand. Under what circumstances is reunification with an existing state deemed an appropriate goal? Are all irredentist claims, by definition, aimed at boundary adjustments? What are the effects of irredentism on the definition of the parent state? To answer these questions, it is necessary to probe much more deeply into the changing objectives of irredentist movements over time.

The fourth issue focuses on the manner in which irredentist claims are presented. Irredentist demands may exist latently for a period of time, without any attempt to realize them (the Moroccan claim to

Spanish Sahara from the mid-1960s to the mid-1970s is a case in point). At other conjunctures specific measures are taken to forward the irredentist aspiration. These might include negotiation, mobilization of the international community or world public opinion, border skirmishes, and outright declarations of war. The strategy and tactics of irredentist ventures, and the differences they exhibit over time, are crucial to an understanding of the dynamics involved and to an evaluation of the patterns of conflict they evoke. Certain measures might induce different types of interactions, which have perceivable domestic and international ramifications and lead to qualitatively distinct results.

A fifth question relates to the manner in which irredentist claims are resolved. Four main outcomes of irredentism have been recorded: (1) the successful readjustment of boundaries to accord with irredentist interests; (2) the redefinition of the bases of group action, usually highlighting separatism at the expense of irredentism; (3) the withdrawal of irredentist demands; (4) the negotiation of a multiplicity of forms of accommodation and compromise. These are aimed at enabling some measure of communal autonomy without altering political sovereignty. In those areas where sophisticated techniques for managing irredentist conflicts have not been developed, irredentist claims may reappear at intervals.

The nature of the solution to irredentist claims may be influenced not only by domestic considerations but also by external involvement. In some cases, a third party has played a key role in imposing a settlement (e.g., the role of the Soviet Union in subduing the irredentist claims among the Balkan states since World War II). In other instances, the overwhelming power of one of the parties in the dispute brought about an enforced termination of the conflict (as in the case of the ability of the United States to allay the Mexican claim for the return of the southwestern states seized in the nineteenth century). In recent years regional organizations and international bodies have had an important role in mediating disputes (e.g., the part played by SEATO in the disputes between Malaysia and Indonesia and between Indonesia and the Philippines or the role of OAU in the Western Sahara and the Horn of Africa). And, of course, legal, diplomatic, and military means have been employed with differing frequencies in specific instances (most recently the international military, economic, and diplomatic campaign to reverse the Iraqi conquest of Kuwait).

The mode of management of irredentist aspirations has thus varied in terms of methods used, parties involved, and agreements reached. Why certain solutions have evolved in some areas and not in others is discussed in the case studies included in this volume.

The sixth major issue raised in relation to irredentist processes concerns policy implications. The termination of a specific dispute

does not necessarily mean that irredentist tendencies are entirely suppressed. An examination of postconflict developments helps to trace
the consequences of alternative resolutions of irredentist conflicts.
Moreover, an analysis of policy ramifications assists in weighing
military, legal, spatial, and structural options more carefully, and
thereby sheds light on the path of irredentism in the future.

The sequence of irredentist processes and the stages they undergo
vary from case to case and from region to region. By looking at the
various facets of irredentism at different phases of irredentist disputes,
the contributors to this book seek to identify the resultant patterns with
greater precision.

International Aspects

Irredentism, by definition, falls into the category of interstate relations.
Irredentist conflicts frequently involve wars, which induce great power
involvement and the intervention of stronger neighboring states. In
many instances irredentist claims have become the topic of debate in
international bodies and have evoked significant concern in the international community.

The external aspects of irredentism warrant close attention and are
therefore highlighted in this volume. First, the role of foreign interests
varies at different points of irredentist processes. The international
involvement at the time of the gestation of irredentist claims, their
mobilization, their presentation, and their termination might have
different causes and quite distinct implications. The authors attempt to
map out these foreign influences and to analyze their implications.

Second, the role of external forces in irredentist disputes has
changed over time. International stances on irredentism have shifted
since the nineteenth century. In the interwar period, general attitudes
(particularly as exhibited in Eastern Europe) were quite different from
in the postwar era (especially vis-à-vis the Third World). The historical mutations in approaches to irredentism have in all probability
affected both the willingness of foreign interests to intervene in
irredentist conflicts and the manner of their involvement. By adopting
a broad historical perspective, this book tries to explore the many facets
of the external dimension of irredentism with greater clarity.

APPROACH

This volume adopts a multidimensional approach to the study of
irredentism and the problematics it entails. The first of these problematics is theoretical: the chapters by Donald Horowitz and Hedva Ben-
Israel focus on the delineation of irredentism and suggest different

ways of understanding its components and dynamics. The second is historical: the contributions by Emanuel Gutmann and by Shalom Reichman and Arnon Golan examine the European experience, highlighting the interplay between state aspirations, cultural claims, and the international environment. The third is comparative: Richard Stoess, Jacob Landau, and Benyamin Neuberger look at the cases of Germany, Turkey, and Africa, respectively, in an effort to reassess the main features of irredentism in the contemporary world. And the fourth problematic is policy oriented: Brian Weinstein examines (as do other authors) some of the connections between official measures and the emergence or suppression of irredentist claims. In the conclusion, Naomi Chazan brings together the findings of the separate contributions and suggests an agenda for future research. These multidisciplinary, historical, and comparative essays thus enable a systematic treatment of irredentism, and suggest some of the intricacies involved in this under-researched phenomenon.

NOTES

1. Gabriel Sheffer, ed., *Modern Diasporas in International Politics* (London: Croom Helm, 1986).
2. Benjamin Akzin, *States and Nations* (New York: Doubleday, 1966).
3. Donald L. Horowitz, *Ethnic Groups in Conflict* (Berkeley and Los Angeles: University of California Press, 1985), p. 281.
4. See Chapter 1 by Donald L. Horowitz.
5. See the difference in views between Donald Horowitz (Chapter 1) and Benyamin Neuberger (Chapter 7) in this volume.

Irredentas and Secessions: Adjacent Phenomena, Neglected Connections

DONALD L. HOROWITZ

To think about something makes it necessary to identify and isolate it, to fix upon it and, in fixing upon it, to reify it. Even before conscious conceptualization occurs, even in the selection of phenomena for study, concepts creep in. The more careful the thinking, the more precise the identification of the phenomena for study, the greater the isolation of one phenomenon from its neighbors, even its near neighbors. When the careful thinker says, "I mean to include *this* and to exclude *that*," the precision that makes any careful thinking possible may come at a price. Less careful but perhaps more nimble thinkers—namely, those actors whose behavior forms the subject of social-science thinking—have a way of putting back together what careful thinkers pull apart.

Secessions and irredentas are near neighbors that can be pulled apart for analysis, properly in my view, but with points of contact and even, at times, a degree of interchangeability that might permit groups to choose one or the other and that also makes it necessary to treat the two phenomena together, in order to have a full view of each. By and large, the two have not been treated together. They have either been treated in isolation or mentioned in the same breath without an appreciation of their connections. When, however, secessions and irredentas are considered together, some rather startling conclusions emerge. Since the two phenomena are sometimes alternatives to each other, the frequency of each is, in part, a function of the frequency of the other. Furthermore, the strength of a given movement may be, in part, a function of the possibility that the alternative movement may arise. Indeed, the fate of a movement, at least in the sense that it manages to extract concessions from a central government, may depend on which course it takes.

TWO DISTINCT PHENOMENA

Secession and irredentism are definable in distinct terms, even if we restrict ourselves solely to ethnically motivated movements. Secession is an attempt by an ethnic group claiming a homeland to withdraw with its territory from the authority of a larger state of which it is a part. Irredentism is a movement by members of an ethnic group in one state to retrieve ethnically kindred people and their territory across borders.

It will quickly be noted that disparate subphenomena are subsumed in the definition of secession propounded here. The definition might be sufficiently elastic to embrace the activity of a group that merely seeks regional autonomy or creation of a federal system and control of its own state as a component of such a system. This was the aim of the Federal party in Sri Lanka until at least 1972 and of the Liberal party in the Sudan until 1958. The same definition of secession might also comprehend the activity of an ethnic group occupying a discrete territory within a state in an existing federal system but aiming to carve a new state out of its portion of the existing state. The Telangana movement in Andhra Pradesh is one of several such movements in India. Nigeria has had many comparable movements, beginning with the United Middle Belt Congress in the 1950s. Finally, and most relevantly for connections to irredentism, this definition of secession certainly includes attempts to form separate, independent, internationally recognized states out of existing sovereign entities, as in the unsuccessful war for Biafra and the successful war for Bangladesh. In this definition, secession thus entails several forms of greater or lesser withdrawal from existing units.

Similarly, irredentism, as defined here, contains two subtypes: the attempt to detach land and people from one state in order to incorporate them in another, as in the case of Somalia's recurrent irredenta against Ethiopia, and the attempt to detach land and people divided among more than one state in order to incorporate them in a single new state— a "Kurdistan," for example, composed of Kurds now living in Iraq, Iran, Syria, and Turkey. Both forms of reconstituted boundaries would qualify as irredentist.

Despite their elasticity, the definitions of the two phenomena are conceptually distinct. Irredentism involves subtracting from one state and adding to another state, new or already existing; secession involves subtracting alone.

Moreover, the distinction between secessions and irredentas seems to capture some important differences in political phenomena on the ground; it is not merely a figment of the imagination of analysts. A glance at the relative frequency of the two phenomena hints at this. There are possibilities aplenty for secession and irredentism in the postcolonial world of Asia, Africa, and the Middle East. Most states are ethnically heterogeneous; of these, most have territorially compact minorities. Likewise, many ethnic groups are divided by territorial boundaries. Consequently, secession and irredentism are both abundantly plausible possibilities in the contemporary world. The necessary conditions, if not the sufficient conditions, for both are present. But the two phenomena are by no means proportionately represented in relation to the possibility of their occurrence. In spite of predictions to the contrary,[1] there have been remarkably few irredentas in the postcolonial states, but there have been a great many secessionist movements.

Withdrawal alone attracts many more adherents to action than does withdrawal coupled with the aim of reincorporation in another state. This seeming puzzle becomes even more perplexing when additional facts are added to the comparison. Consider just two. First, although secession is common, the victory of secessionist movements is extremely uncommon. Victory requires external assistance, which is rarely forthcoming in a volume and duration sufficient to win the war and create the new secessionist state. The Bangladesh example is conspicuous by its exceptional character. The improbability of success, however, has not deterred a significant number of secessionist groups. Second—again contrary to forecasts that wealthy regions would be more likely secessionists[2]—secessionist regions are disproportionately ill favored in resources and per capita income.[3] Not infrequently, groups attempt to withdraw from states from which their region actually receives a subsidy.

Counterintuitively, then, in numbers that are both absolute and relative to the possibilities, secession is much more frequent than irredentism, and this despite the enormous obstacles to success and the disadvantages most secessionist regions would face were they to succeed. By contrast, irredentism is rare, even though the first subtype of the definition of irredentism would usually involve the armed forces of one state in retrieving kinsmen across borders from another. Although irredentism would often carry with it military resources often denied secessionists, that advantage does not appear to increase the frequency of irredentas. Some behavioral features must therefore be associated with one phenomenon that are not associated with the other. Otherwise, the disparate incidence of the two phenomena cannot be explained.

This suffices to demonstrate the utility of distinguishing between secessions and irredentas. In fact, there is a whole spectrum of phenomena worth distinguishing. At one end, there are international border disputes that have no ethnic component and are therefore not irredentist. Latin American history is filled with such disputes.[4] At the other end of the spectrum, there are territorially compact groups that nevertheless do not wholly dominate their region, which is ethnically heterogeneous. Although they may not aspire to secession, they may well aspire to homogeneity and take violent steps toward that end. A good many ethnic riots produce a stream of refugees of the victim group, which in turn fosters increased territorial segregation. Violence that increases homogenization is, to be sure, a frequent prelude to secession or irredentism—it may be that for the Albanians in the Kosovo province of Yugoslavia,[5] but it need not be and probably is not for groups like the Assamese in India.

Having delimited the two phenomena and argued that, on the face of it, the delimitation seems useful, I now propose to put back together what I have pulled apart. I adhere to the utility of the secession-irredentism distinction, and I continue to think the differential incidence of the two is partly explicable in terms that are peculiar to the dynamics of each.[6] Nevertheless, I intend to show that there are some fairly close connections between the two as well. For example, one reason there are few irredentas may be that many groups that have a choice between irredentism and secession find the latter the more satisfying choice. Indeed, the potential for irredentism may increase the frequency and strength of secession, but not vice versa. In short, while it makes a difference which course of action a group is embarked upon, my aim here is to elucidate the neglected interrelations between secessions and irredentas where both are possible.

TWO RELATED PHENOMENA

The connections between secessionist and irredentist movements can be divided into three sets of issues. The first relates to the convertibility of the two types of movement. The second involves the relative frequency of secessions and irredentas. The third concerns the relative strength of the movements. These three issues are, as we shall see, closely related to each other.

The Convertibility of Claims

To speak seriously of interchangeability—of the possibility that a movement may become either secessionist or irredentist or that it may move from one category to the other—is to limit ourselves to those territorially compact ethnic groups that span borders. Not all secessionists are in this category. Bengalis are found on the Indian side of the border as well as on what is now the Bangladesh side and what was before 1971 the East Pakistan side, but Ibo (except for some migrants to other countries) are entirely contained within Nigeria's boundaries. The Bengalis might have become either irredentist or secessionist, but the Ibo had no irredentist option. Although a great many groups do span borders, a good many others are in the Ibo category.

Violence is frequently convertible from one form to another. Countries that experience political violence of one sort are likely to experience violence of another sort.[7] Relatively spontaneous violence often gives way at later stages to more organized violence. Riots, for example, are a common forerunner of secessionist movements. For transborder ethnic groups, it stands to reason that if conditions are not propitious for irredentism, those groups may turn to secession, and vice versa.

Underpinning the convertibility of movements is the mutability of ethnic-group claims, of international relations, and of transborder ethnic affinities.   Groups (and states) are not born irredentist or secessionist. They can and do move back and forth from integrated participation in the state of which they are a part to a posture of secession or irredentism.

To begin with, whether a group is integrationist or secessionist depends, in large measure, on its assessment of its prospects in the undivided state. The Ibo were the most prominent proponents of one Nigeria. With a considerable investment in human capital, they had migrated all over Nigeria in their quest for employment. Perhaps one Ibo in four or five lived outside the Eastern Region before 1966. But when recurrent violence, culminating in the massacres of September–October 1966, drove the Ibo back to the east, then and then only did the Ibo become secessionist. Meanwhile, the Hausa traveled in the opposite direction, from their openly secessionist inclinations of mid-1966 to their strong role in suppressing the Biafra secession and preserving an undivided Nigeria.

The Ibo and Hausa were not alone in altering their collective objectives. The Sri Lankan Tamils are as reluctant a group of secessionists as may be found, but secessionist some did become, especially after the bloody anti-Tamil riots of 1983. The southern Sudanese, on the other hand, were divided and, even when not divided, were ambiguous about what they wanted during the civil war of 1963–1972. For some groups, the dominant theme was a settlement within the Sudan; for others, it was southern independence. At times, one or another of these themes was ascendant; at other times, both were heard simultaneously, even from the same speaker. In 1972, an abrupt settlement of the war, on terms of regional autonomy, was reached. Following the resumption of hostilities in the southern Sudan in the 1980s, guerrillas fighting in the south declared as their goal the democratization of the entire country, rather than merely the liberation of the southern Sudan. Like the Nigerians, the southern Sudanese have, at various times, moved in various directions.

That flexibility extends to irredentism. It is no secret that many Kurds advocate the creation of a Kurdistan out of portions of several independent states. During most of the post–World War II period, however, regional autonomy and secession, rather than irredentism, have been the stated Kurdish objectives.[8] There is an obvious reason for this. Kurds in Iraq have required assistance from Iran to make any claim effective. From time to time, Iran has provided substantial aid. Without any doubt, no such aid could be expected for a movement that pursued the irredentist objective of unification of all the Kurds, including those in Iran.

To put the point sharply, the propensity for an irredentist ideology to emerge among an ethnic group to be retrieved is directly related to the likelihood that the putative irredentist state will espouse a similar irredentist ideology. That propensity is inversely related to the likelihood that the emergence of an irredentist claim will produce denial of the international assistance that would be accorded to secessionists or, even worse, will produce suppression of the irredentists.

To make matters more complex, it is not merely ethnic groups that are fickle in their objectives. State policies supporting or opposing secessions and irredentas also change. In 1975, Iran abruptly terminated military assistance to Kurds in Iraq and eventually closed its border to them, thereby dooming their movement. In 1987, India ceased its assistance to Sri Lankan Tamil secessionists, reached an agreement with the Sri Lankan government providing for Tamil regional autonomy instead, and attempted to suppress by force armed Tamil guerrillas in Sri Lanka itself. Periodically, Somalia, perhaps the most persistently irredentist state in the postcolonial world, has embarked upon a policy of détente with Ethiopia, which at other times is the target of its irredenta. State policy in pursuit of irredentism tends to be inconstant.

That inconstancy drives some potential irredentists to secession instead. For a time in the 1970s, it seemed as if the connections between the Malaysian state of Sabah and the Moro National Liberation Front (MNLF) in the Philippines might support an attempt to link the two politically. The ethnic identity of the chief minister of Sabah was Suluk, as was that of a good many Philippine Muslims engaged in the combat, and the chief minister had relatives across what had always been a permeable water boundary. But there are Malaysians of Suluk origin only in Sabah, and they are a distinct minority even there. No leaders in Kuala Lumpur were Suluk. Eventually, the chief minister was voted out of office, and the remote possibility of irredentism was stillborn. The MNLF never turned its struggle in an irredentist direction.

The southern Philippine example brings us to one final aspect of convertibility: the convertibility of ethnic affinities. To define irredentism as an attempt to retrieve kindred people across boundaries is to assume that kindred people know each other, that kinship and ethnicity are firm. It is by now well established, however, that ethnic identity is variable over time and over context. Consider, for example, the case of Malays in southern Thailand. There is no doubt whatever that migration and interchange between them and Malays in the northern Malaysian states of Kedah and Kelantan have been considerable, and there are still family ties across the border.[9] To most Malays, however, the "Pattani Malays" of southern Thailand seem rather foreign, and their distance is accentuated by the Indonesian origin of many Malays in southern Malaysian states. One of the major problems with irredentism is that the ethnic affinity of the core of a putative irredentist state may not extend to people at and beyond the periphery, and those are the very people who are to be retrieved.

The Relative Frequency of Movements

Like some of the other forces conducive to the convertibility of movements, the variability of group affinities across borders extends also to the relative frequency of secessionist and irredentist claims. Because of the common reluctance of people at the center to see nominally kindred people on the periphery as truly members of the same ethnic group, and for many other reasons as well, irredentist action on the part of the potential retrieving state is distinctly uncommon. I shall not rehearse all of these reasons here, because they have been laid out carefully elsewhere.[10] I shall merely touch on a few that bear on the comparative frequency of secessions and irredentas.

For several reasons, the foreign-policy goals of most putative irredentist states (apart from the actual goal of retrieval) can be achieved better by encouraging secessionist movements by groups located in antagonistic states than by encouraging irredentism. For one thing, there is the easy reversibility of the policy. As the Iranians demonstrated in 1975, aid to secessionists can be terminated abruptly in return for a quid pro quo. Carefully rationed Malaysian assistance to the Moro secessionists in the Philippines helped persuade the Philippine government to abandon its claim on the Malaysian state of Sabah. Ethiopia has helped southern Sudanese secessionists in order to discourage Sudanese help for secessionists in Ethiopia. Typically, when the objectives are achieved, the aid is terminated—which is one reason why there are many wars fought by secessionists but few that they win. Even the government of India was able to reverse its policy of support for the Tamil secessionists in Sri Lanka in return for a regional autonomy agreement. The Sri Lankan Tamils are a kindred people, which many secessionists who receive aid are not,[11] but there was no irredentist claim advanced in their behalf. Aid to irredentists, however, is underpinned by an ideology of common fate that hardly lends itself to abrupt termination. Indeed, when the Somali regime did disengage from war in the Ogaden, the decision helped precipitate the Somali coup of 1969, because kindred groups in the armed forces did not wish to abandon

Somalis of the Darood subgroup on the Ethiopian side of the border.

If adjacent states find irredentism unattractive, the feeling is reciprocated by many discontented, territorially compact, transborder ethnic groups. Groups like these, with the potential to be retrieved, find retrieval by the putative irredentist state undesirable. This may be because that state is poorer or less prestigious or more authoritarian than the state in which they are now encapsulated. Baluch would rather be in Pakistan or be independent than be in Afghanistan, even if Afghanistan were at peace. Toubou in northern Chad might equally prefer several alternative fates to merger in Qaddafi's Libya. Ethnic affinity across borders is not enough by itself to make merger attractive.

One reason fostering the reluctance to be incorporated is so obvious that it has escaped notice altogether: the interests of political leaders of a potentially secessionist region. They are generally willing to accept independence, even though independence often means an economic position for their state that is inferior to the one it enjoyed as part of an undivided state, partly because with independence they will no longer have to compete for leadership positions with all the other political leaders in the undivided state. By partitioning their area within sovereign boundaries, they also keep out competition for leadership. The ready willingness of so many backward regions to attempt secession soon after independence owes something to the interests of leaders who felt unable to compete in the wider arena.

The same logic applies to the response to the prospect of annexation in an adjacent, albeit ethnically kindred, state. Irredentism will re-merge not just populations but leadership pools. True enough, the ethnic affinities of the annexing and the annexed peoples may be more felicitous, but for leaders this may be more, rather than less, dangerous. If there is a sharp disparity of ethnic identification between the population of a given region and the population of the rest of the state in which it is currently merged, leaders of the group dominant in the region at least face no external challenge to their leadership of that group from leaders of the population in the remainder of the undivided state; by the same token, they are unable to aspire to leadership positions in the undivided state. This is the presecession situation. In the postsecession situation, those leaders still face no external challenge to their leadership, but now their group leadership becomes state leadership, for the region has achieved sovereignty. If, instead of secession, the choice is merger into an existing, adjacent state via irredentism, regional leaders have not achieved sovereignty and also are no longer immune from external challenge. Quite the opposite. Ethnic affinities across the irredentist border open the way to challenges to their leadership from ethnically kindred leaders of the annexing state.

There are also, of course, wider opportunities for leaders of the annexed region in the larger irredentist state as a whole, but these are more circumscribed than they might at first appear. First, leaders from the newly annexed region must break into what is likely to be a crystallized political situation and do so from a merely regional base, with at best imperfect knowledge of the new state and its political patterns. Second, because ethnic affinities are rarely undifferentiated, the newly annexed area stands every chance of being regarded as at least subethnically different in composition (in dialect, accent, family ties, or customs)—in short, as truly peripheral[12]—and its people, cousins though they are, are likely to be viewed as rustics who lived too long under an alien regime. So the position of the annexed region as peripheral newcomer is an enormous impediment to the national-level ambitions of its leaders, should irredentism succeed.

Given this structure of opportunities and constraints, is it not obvious that secession will be the preferred alternative of most ethnic leaders in separatist regions? Of course, leadership interests are not always overriding. Leaders may be, and sometimes are, overruled by an avalanche of mass ethnic sentiment.[13] Moreover, the particular structure of opportunities and constraints will vary from one situation to another, and some regional leaders may prefer irredentism to secession, just as many prefer continuation of the region in the undivided state of which it is currently a part.[14] But where withdrawal from that state is the preferred option, most leaders, most of the time, will think in terms of becoming leaders of the sovereign state, rather than risking reincorporation into another, larger state, the behavior of which toward a newly annexed region is, in any case, impossible to foretell. Overall, leadership interests are a major explanation for the frequency of secession and the infrequency of irredentas.

Reluctance to be annexed by an adjacent state may also derive from the heterogeneity of the irredentist state. Even assuming transborder ethnic affinities are intact, the retrieving state may contain a plurality of ethnic groups, so that a decision in favor of irredentism will not necessarily be a decision resulting in ethnic self-determination, much less domination in the new state. The Ewe and the Bakongo are in this position. Even if adjoining states containing other Ewe and Bakongo wished to retrieve them—which they do not—the presence of still other powerful ethnic groups in the retrieving state would deter acceptance of the offer.

Moreover, such potentially irredentist groups—the Kurds are also among them—cannot practically go the alternative route and opt for multiple secessions, carving out of several existing states a new, homogeneous Ewe, Bakongo, or Kurdish state. One secession is difficult enough; it has long odds. But multiple secessions threaten the very governments whose aid across borders is the indispensable component of success. I have already noted the unwillingness of the Kurds in Iraq to take a position regarding Kurds in Iran that would have precluded Iranian assistance. The same applies to all such transborder groups. For this reason, potential irredentists are much more likely to engage in their own separate secessions.

As a matter of fact, virtually everything I have said thus far points in the same direction. If claims are convertible from secession to irredenta and vice versa, if transborder affinities are imperfectly developed, if state policy is at best inconstant, and if there is frequently a reluctance to retrieve or to be retrieved, the sum of all of this is a powerful structural bias against the incidence of irredentism. What that means is that discontented groups will tend to look favorably on secession, rather than on irredentism, where both are possible. The Malays of southern Thailand, who might have become irredentist but find no such invitation from across the Malaysian border, are likely to find secession an attractive alternative. As noted earlier, the many compact groups that do not span borders do not, by definition, have an irredentist option. In practice, neither do most of the many transborder groups have an irredentist option.

In short, all else being equal, the fewer the irredentas, the larger the number of secessionist movements. And since irredentas are rare, secession is by far the more frequent movement of territorially compact ethnic groups. The opposite conclusion also seems likely: ceteris paribus, if for some reason the various inhibitions on irredentism were to decline and irredentism were to become more common, there would also be fewer secessionists.

That is not to say that there is only a finite amount of ethnic discontent available or a finite number of movements possible among territorially compact ethnic groups. It is only to make the important point that the two types of movement are closely related and frequently are plausible alternatives to each other. The behavior of many groups in one direction or another is structured by the availability or absence of the other option. Since there is no reason to think the inhibitions on irredentism will in fact decline—particularly because irredentism, unlike secession, depends on the presence of two willing parties whose interests and affinities are rarely identical—secession is likely to remain by far the more common movement.

The Strength of Movements

The strength of secessionist and irredentist movements—and their prospects for success—may be affected in various ways by whether they choose one or the other alternative and by whether the other possibility lurks in the background. If a transborder group attempts secession, the states hosting its population may combine to suppress the movement, as Iran and Pakistan have both suppressed the Baluch movement. If the groups adjacent to the border choose separate secessions at different times, the neighboring governments may, on the contrary, provide assistance to the secessionists in the country across the border, on the Ethiopia-Sudan model. If, on the other hand, a movement becomes irredentist and one of the transborder segments seeks incorporation in the neighboring state, it is quite possible that the two states will be at war over this issue.[15] So the range of possibilities simultaneously affects prospects for the discontented ethnic groups and for relations between the states of which they are a part. The form of the movement thus has consequences, and the likely consequences presumably have a reciprocal influence on the form the movement takes and the objectives it proclaims.

Whether secessionists receive any significant support from the state across the border will depend, in considerable measure, on the international interests of that state and its objectives with respect to its neighbor. Where interests are perceived to be in conflict, at least some help can generally be expected, as Pakistan's receptivity to the Sikh independence movement shows. But where irredentism is in the background—even in the very remote background, as in India's relations to the Sri Lankan Tamils (despite Sinhalese suspicions of worse)—more support can be expected, at least for a time. Indeed, because of external help of various kinds, from various sources, both the Sikh and the Sri Lankan Tamil movements engaged in armed warfare far out of proportion to the underlying and at best ambivalent sentiments of their putatively secessionist populations. The armed militants had their way because of international connections.

Where, however, irredentist sentiment is more strongly felt in the putative retrieving state, warfare may be initiated even if—and perhaps *because*—the authorities in the putative irredentist state are unsympathetic to the irredentist objective. I am thinking here of the warfare that made Bangladesh independent. To be sure, there were several reasons why India intervened in East Bengal in 1971. There was an unparalleled opportunity to dismember Pakistan and install a friendlier government on the eastern frontier. There was the burden of refugees and the prospect of long-simmering guerrilla warfare across borders under circumstances that might later become more favorable to Pakistan. Pakistan's retaliation for inevitable Indian assistance to the guerrillas might prove painful. But, above and beyond all the other reasons, there were incipient claims in West Bengal for the unification of all Bengalis, east and west. Had this movement succeeded, the Hindu-Muslim balance in India would have been altered permanently, and India would have assumed the burden of supporting a very poor dependent state. An independent Bangladesh was far preferable to a growing demand for a Bengali irredenta. Consequently, India's willingness to go to war to secure Bangladesh's independence was likely colored by the alternative (and undesirable) possibility of irredentism. The success of the war produced a fait accompli, an independent Bangladesh that ended the irredentist clamor the government of India had no wish to encourage.

If this analysis is correct, it shows that the only successful secession in the post–World War II period was the result of a secessionist war conducted in the growing shadow of a potential irredenta.[16] And if this is so, the example shows again, not merely how the two phenomena are related, but how the reluctance of states to espouse irredentist claims drives ethnic movements toward secession—in this case, secession augmented by military force that an irredenta-shy regime committed in time to forestall an irredentist movement it had no wish to encourage.

THE CHOICE OF MOVEMENT AND THE BASES OF ACTION

In explaining the relationship between secessions and irredentas, I have not gone all the way back to account for the emergence of movements for ethnoterritorial separatism in the first instance. To do this would require much greater explication of the course of ethnic relations within the undivided state. There is now quite a wide range of theorizing on the emergence of such movements, some more inward looking, emphasizing intraethnic history, myths of origin, and connections to land, others more outward looking, emphasizing interethnic changes within the present territory.[17] What is rare is a general theory that accounts for whether ethnoterritorial separatism will take a secessionist or irredentist course. The two are typically bracketed together in the literature, as if the emergence of one or the other were a matter of no consequence or a happenstance event.

We have seen, however, that secessions and irredentas are convertible under some circumstances but not perfectly interchangeable at all. Their widely differential frequency shows how much more attractive secession is overall. To the participants, it obviously matters enormously which course is chosen, and it follows that the conditions associated with each course can, in principle, be specified. As they make such choices, group members and leaders resort to an array of perceptual and calculative considerations. Who are our true cousins? In which territorial unit are my political ambitions more likely to be fulfilled? Who will deploy force against us if we go in one direction or another? Neither secession nor irredentism is a spontaneous, unorganized movement, so it is hardly surprising that the strategic choice should have a heavy overlay of calculations of rational interest.

Such a conclusion should not, however, displace the role of the emotional discomfort that is customarily felt in conflict-prone inter-ethnic relations or the perceptions of ethnic affinity and disparity that define group boundaries—neither of which is properly subsumed in any sensible scheme based wholly on rational interest. Indeed, even as we explain the preference for secession over irredentism on understandable calculative grounds, we elide an element of choice that belies the dominant role of calculation: if nearly every secession is doomed to failure, why do secessionist movements continue to arise? Until we are able to specify the mix of givens and chosens, of passionate and calculative behavior, with greater precision, we shall continue to bracket related ethnic phenomena, the choice of which is neither an unpredictable event nor a matter of indifference to the participants.

NOTES

1. Rupert Emerson, *From Empire to Nation* (Cambridge, Mass.: Harvard University Press, 1960), p. 105.
2. Immanuel Wallerstein, *Africa: The Politics of Independence* (New York: Vintage, 1961), p. 88.
3. Donald L. Horowitz, "Patterns of Ethnic Separatism," *Comparative Studies in Society and History* 23, 2 (April 1981): 165–195, at p. 194.
4. As Jacob Landau pointed out at the conference from which this volume emerged.
5. See Brian Weinstein, Chapter 8.
6. Donald L. Horowitz, *Ethnic Groups in Conflict* (Berkeley and Los Angeles: University of California Press, 1985), ch. 6, "The Logic of Secessions and Irredentas."
7. Ted Robert Gurr, *Why Men Rebel* (Princeton, N. J.: Princeton University Press, 1970), pp. 4–5.
8. Joane Nagel, "The Conditions of Ethnic Separatism: The Kurds in Turkey, Iran, and Iraq," *Ethnicity* 7, 3 (September 1980): 279–297; George S. Harris, "Ethnic Conflict and the Kurds," *The Annals* 433 (September 1977): 112–124.
9. David J. Banks, *Malay Kinship* (Philadelphia: Institute for the Study of Human Issues, 1983), pp. 25–28.
10. Horowitz, *Ethnic Groups in Conflict*, pp. 281–288, a section entitled "Irredentism: Prerogative of the Few."
11. Ibid., pp. 274–275.
12. This is not necessarily a reflection of the actual historical role of the region now regarded as peripheral. As Emanuel Gutmann points out in Chapter 3, Alsace is the cradle of medieval history, as well as the site of German humanism and the German Renaissance. This has not prevented German historians from attempting to belittle the historical importance of

Alsace and to portray it as peripheral.

13. Here, however, it should be borne in mind that the leadership interests are likely to be disproportionately important. Once the matter comes down to secession or irredentism, it will probably also come to fighting, and the leaders will negotiate access to the crucial arms.

14. For a discussion of the many African groups divided by boundaries, see A. I. Asiwaju, ed., *Partitioned Africans* (New York: St. Martin's Press, 1985).

15. This point is based on Myron Weiner's comments at the conference from which this volume emerged.

16. Some might argue that the partition of Cyprus in 1974 was a second case of successful secession. If so, it shares many of the properties of the Bangladesh case, especially the external invasion from a state that, had it not helped set up an autonomous Turkish state on Cyprus, might have come under pressure to annex the Turkish areas of the island.

17. Compare, for example, Anthony D. Smith, *The Ethnic Revival in the Modern World* (Cambridge: Cambridge University Press, 1981), pp. 64–66, with Ronald Rogowski, "Causes and Varieties of Nationalism: A Rationalist Account," in Ronald Rogowski and Edward A. Tiryakian, eds., *New Nationalisms of the Developed West* (Boston: George Allen & Unwin, 1985), pp. 87–107.

CHAPTER 2

Irredentism: Nationalism Reexamined

HEDVA BEN-ISRAEL

I should like to make some historical points about irredentism based mainly on the study of the interwar period. The term irredentism is, I think, sometimes used far too loosely to denote any claim for the return or acquisition of territory. Such usage can be misleading. The literature on irredentism includes an article entitled "The British Attitude Towards Germany's Colonial Irredentism in Africa in the Inter-War Years"[1]—I thought this was a joke. Even if any German government had felt strongly about the return of its colonies, "irredentism" would not have described its policy. The strongest arguments for the return of Germany's colonies to her as a matter of justice as well as expediency were made at one time or another in Britain. One of the times that Hitler alluded to colonies was in a 1936 speech in which he sneered at the idea that they had any other purpose than that of exploitation in which Germany was entitled to share.[2]

Irredentism is usually expressed by a different category of rhetoric. The closest the German advocates of the return of the colonies ever came to a vocabulary of rights was when they condemned the reason given for the confiscation of the colonies, namely, the German maltreatment of natives, as the "colonial-guilt lie," to be rejected along with the better-known "war-guilt lie." Because Germany was the expansionist power of the interwar period it might be pointed out that irredentism is a term that would eminently suit the policy of the Weimar Republic toward the Polish border, corridor, and so on. Here we have the case of Germans having been torn away from the mother country along with the territory they lived on and put under Polish sovereignty. The irredentist aim of retrieving them was the constant policy of all German governments before Hitler. It also marked a continuation of the traditional anti-Polish orientation of military and conservative circles in Prussia that, in this respect, survived in Weimar Germany and later in the conservative anti-Nazi opposition.

On the other hand, the expansionist Nazi government was in fact the least "irredentist." More even than the conservative opposition, Hitler was ready to accommodate Poland for the sake of support against Russia before he turned to the opposite policy. One could say his approach continued a traditional Austrian rather than Prussian policy. In any case, especially in secret meetings, for internal purposes the rationale of Nazi German expansion was always the defense not of any group of Germans but of the German *Volk* as a whole—the territories it needed, its economic standard, and its rightful status in the world. We shall have to come back to this point again.

WHAT IS IRREDENTISM?

The key aspect of irredentism, I would suggest, is the tension between land and people. Irredentism is not just any claim for annexing territory, or even adjacent territory with a kin population in it, although this is sometimes the case. Irredentism pertains in the first place to territory demanded by a state on the ground that it had been or should have been an integral part of the national heritage. Ethnic populations often come into it, but it is, in my opinion, territory more than population that is central in irredentist movements, and this distinguishes irredentist from pan movements.

South Tyrol, the outstanding case of irredentism, was claimed by the Italians although their people were in a minority there.[3] The same region was cheerfully abandoned by Hitler even though Germans were in a majority there. The 1939 Pact of Steel was accompanied by a realistic solution: a forced plebiscite to be followed by either forced assimilation or forced emigration of Germans, all agreed to by Hitler. Italian irredentism for South Tyrol before World War I was based on historic rights and, of course, strategic interests.[4] On the other hand, after World War II Austria developed toward South Tyrol an authentic irredentism accompanied by all the necessary accoutrements of bombs, terror, and so on. South Tyrol remained Italian, although largely autonomous, because in the tension between territorial demands and population demands the former carried the day. The notion of redeeming a certain territory for the nation can mean acquiring land even without kinsmen on it, and perhaps even clear of the alien populations inhabiting it. If the Italians in their newly unified independent state did not have just such a concept of land in mind in making further territorial claims, they would not have chosen, in the late 1870s, the term "Italia Irredenta," so laden not only with the biblical connotation of redeeming a land for a people but also with the Mazzinian political and religious ideology of individual and national redemption through the liberation of the national land. They meant to invest further territorial expansion with the same aura of an elevated national effort as the rest of the Risorgimento.

Greek irredentism preceded that of the Italians because their modern state was set up earlier. The irredentist urge that the Greeks manifestly had, but for which the word irredentism did not yet exist, they called the Great Dream or the Megali Idea.[5] What they meant by it was the renewal of the Byzantine Empire, and, of course, the sine qua non of their aspirations was the appropriation of Constantinople. They had to have Constantinople just as the Italians had to have Rome and the Jews Jerusalem. The grounds were not ethnic or linguistic, although in the case of Italy they could also be those. That is because the grounds did not relate in the first place to populations but to territories that had historical and religious significance. By the time Greek irredentist aspirations reached uncontainable proportions (being also an internal matter of mass mobilization), and were exploded with the help of external intervention, the term irredentism had already been invented. Historians could refer to early Greek aspirations as irredentist without being anachronistic, for the substance was there, including the denigration of the present state in comparison with the Great Dream. There was also the combination of mysticism and rapaciousness with which an irredentist situation is inevitably accompanied.

It seems no accident that the three modern national movements that were most preoccupied with the idea of the redemption of land, and that became models of irredentism to others, are the three modern nationalisms that in the nineteenth century claimed to revive the three ancient civilizations of the Western world in their historical setting. They were best able to infuse what to others may seem a sheer need for a territorial base, with arguments resounding with history and religion. The notion of hallowed ground seems inherent in the verbalization of irredentism as a political aim. Today, in adopting the term for technical usage in political and historical discourse, we do well to drop the inflated rhetoric, of course, but at the same time to retain a precise connotation that differentiates irredentism from other available terms for national policies or aspirations aimed at territorial expansion.

THE CASE OF CZECHOSLOVAKIA

The case I should like to look at closely for elements of irredentism is that of the German regions in Bohemia, the celebrated object of the 1938 Munich agreement. It is often uncritically assumed to be a classical case of German irredentism—a result, perhaps, of a tendency, sometimes unwitting, to characterize historical changes merely by their consequences.

The case of the Bohemian Germans is more complex than that of the Germans under Polish rule in the interwar period, which was already cited as a straightforward case of irredentism. In Bohemia there was an old history of Czechs and Germans living together, both mixed and separated, locked in an ambiguous relationship that included both mutual assimilation and profound hostility. As a type of national situation, it is most similar to that of Ireland. In both cases, and at about the same time in the early modern period, an ancient people with memories of independent kingship and heroic deeds and with pride in past contributions to European civilization were conquered and oppressed by a neighboring empire, had their aristocratic and bourgeois leadership eliminated or exiled, and had their peasantry enslaved. In both cases, separate national identities were fostered through colonization and religious wars as well as through class distinctions. In both cases, ethnic relations were ambiguous on every level, with opposites such as total assimilation and total separatism existing in proximity. The Czechs, like the Irish, were a conquered nation that continued to live in its historic homeland. Attachment to the land was therefore taken for granted; it was attachment to the culture that became an issue the more assimilation gained ground. In the Czech as in the Irish case (as indeed in other cases not as similar in other respects), the cultural revival was inspired by a will to salvage and foster a separate identity.

Everything said so far pertains to the growth and development of the national movement and has nothing to do with irredentism—precisely because the territorial base was not in question. In Ireland the question of boundaries and the resulting irredentism arose with partition. For stirrings of irredentism in the case of the Czech national movement, we have to look into the period during World War I when the Czech leadership switched from its demands, persistent since the nineteenth century, for ethnic and regional autonomy (a sort of Home Rule idea) within a reformed and restructured Hapsburg empire or federation, to the new demand for absolute national sovereignty. When attention moved from the people to the land, from cultural and political autonomy for the Czech people to a Czech sovereign state within its own defined and defensible borders, then and only then were irredentist aims conceived and broadcast. When the issue became one of an incipient state, the question of the extent of territory became all important. It is here that we can watch irredentism following in the wake of mere nationalism. Ethnic regions would have sufficed for the autonomous Czechs, but there was no way a viable state could have been set up without the voluntary inclusion of the Slovaks and the involuntary inclusion of the German and other minorities. When it became clear to the Czech leaders that they should be bidding for independence, they started propagating the demand for the historical lands of the crown of St. Wenceslaw, for the historical frontiers. Fortunately for the success of their argumentation, the ancient frontiers were in their case also the strategic and economic frontiers, although not, of course, the ethnic ones.[6]

In the declaration of sovereignty of October 28, 1918,[7] Bohemia, Moravia, and Silesia were included on the ground of the historical wholeness of the Czech lands, and when the Supreme Council accepted and explained these frontiers, it reiterated the Czech argument to the degree of justifying even the inclusion of alien populations on historical grounds. This would allow, they said, the Germans and other minorities to collaborate with the Czechs in developing the national unity that history had bestowed upon them.

In other words, the Anglo-Saxon idea of a nation as created by a state was grafted onto a central European scene of rival national movements competing for the right to create a state on one and the same territory. This was not a likely ideological basis for a successful multiethnic state, but it does give an early glimpse of a reality that became so important later. The Allied friends of the new states never really accepted the idea of the state belonging to one nation ruling over minorities, a development that later turned them against the successor states.

If we turn to look for irredentism among the Germans thus included in the Czech state, we find them in 1918 evoking self-determinism more than their right to the land. Self-determinism was the main principle at work and it was their obvious straw to cling to. The only power that had the right and did raise authentic irredentist claims over the German regions of Bohemia was, of course, Austria, which no longer had a common border except with one of the four regions populated by the Germans.

The German minority in Bohemia had for centuries been the favored nation if not the ruling caste. Faced with inclusion in a new Czechoslovak state, it protested loudly. Like the unionists in Northern Ireland whenever Home Rule was approaching, they were, through the fear of becoming a second-class minority in a new national state, the first to try and break away through demonstrative and revolutionary action. In their declaration of independence of October 21, 1918, for instance, the Germans claimed to be setting up an independent German-Austrian state. Few of their declarations mentioned annexation to Austria or Germany. In the south, a sparsely inhabited forest region did declare the intention of joining Austria. There were, on the other hand, military voices in Germany calling for an enforced annexation to Germany of the Austrian areas of Bohemia. Was all this a form of German irredentism? Certainly the Austrian demand was, in spite of the absence of a common border, irredentist. After all, East Prussia remained German even though it was separated from the rest of Germany by the Polish corridor. To choose to belong to Germany, on the other hand, was an act of self-determination, or of support for Anschluss on the old line of Pan-Germanism or the *Mittel-europa* idea, long advocated in the Austrian Empire by nationalist and socialist parties, especially in mixed areas such as Bohemia.

It seems possible, on the basis of German Bohemian claims, to make a case for the view that the Bohemian Germans were, more than anything, separatists and not an irredentist minority seeking annexation. They were, in fact, voicing a Bohemian German nationalism and a demand for self-determination that would affirm their national rights in their country and prevent the setting up of a Czech state in which they would end up as a national minority, which is exactly what happened.

As to their later position in the Czech state, it is a fair summary of the evidence to say that the Czechs tried to reconcile their own aim of being masters in their own house with that of doing justice by their minorities, but not, of course, as much justice as they themselves had demanded from the Hapsburg state. The tone was given by Masaryk in the new parliament in December 1918 when he spoke of immigrants and colonists and also said that the land was Czech and that Czechs would no longer be abandoned to German culture. Soon after, he averred that the Czechs were the "state's nation" and the Germans were the pioneer colonizers, adding ominously that the Czechs had only this one land whereas the Germans had other lands. That all this was said by the most revered and humanistic of all modern liberal nationalists does at least bring out the strength of poststatehood territorial irredentism in Czech nationalism. I purposely used the term irredentism here even though there was no question of demanding further annexations of territory to the state, because, in fact, the Czechs were practicing a sort of irredentist policy within their own territory.

The Czechs possessed the German regions of Bohemia just as the Italians possessed South Tyrol. In both cases, the state ruled over a region in which the majority was alien and reluctant to be included in the state. In the case of the Bohemian Germans, there was at first noncooperation, boycotting of elections, and the like for some years. In the case of South Tyrol, Mussolini declared proudly that he was forcing assimilation. "We have settled colonists," he said, "and we are imposing the Italian language." The Czechs, on the other hand, truly devoted to democratic ways, declared opposite intentions, promising and indeed extending language rights and working toward cultural autonomy, a certain regional decentralization, and proportional sharing in government posts through a minorities law that would ensure these rights.

The result was nevertheless the same in both cases. In carrying out agrarian reform, which in all the new states was a means of achieving social aims through nationally inspired expropriation, the Czech government did transfer about a third of the lands previously owned by Germans to Czech settlers, partly exservicemen, as was done in Italy.

This was, of course, because the large estates now divided had belonged to German landlords, the ascendancy of Hapsburg times. In dividing the large estates, however, there seems to have been an ethnic as well as an agrarian result. New Czech settlers in German regions brought with them the right to Czech-language schools, courts, officials, and so on. Colonization, settlement, and denationalization became increasingly interchangeable terms in the German lists of grievances and in the German nationalist rhetoric, which in itself became a lever for further distrust and discrimination. A very similar situation had been familiar in the German industrial towns in Bohemia for at least a generation. There, toward the end of the nineteenth century, German industrial workers had organized to prevent the migration of Czech former peasants into the cities, where they competed for jobs and took lower wages. The socialist unions led the campaign for discrimination on ethnic grounds. Now, under different circumstances, the Czech government was engineering Czech agrarian settlements, and the Germans protested as before. Reclaiming the land for the Czech nation was an irredentist activity par excellence whether it affected external policy or, for the time being, only internal relations.

Other stock grievances of the Germans in Czechoslovakia were discrimination in the distribution of government contracts and of unemployment and welfare subsidies. The economic nature of most German complaints against the Czech officials and government was a natural result of the fact that personal prejudices and preferences were most likely to affect decisions on the economic level, especially as regards welfare and subsidies. But there was also an initial flaw built into the economic structure of the state. A highly industrialized area that had been the industrial heart of an empire was oversized for the Czech state. This in itself caused more hardship among the Germans, who were the majority in the industrial areas. When the economic crisis limited international trade even further, and the new Nazi state embarked on an autarkic system, many German exporting firms in Bohemia, whether in glass, textiles, or tourism, suffered disproportionately to the rest of the economy. This added to German discontent and gave enough of a truthful ring to German complaints about discrimination to make even wild propaganda credible.

But the main interest, to be sure, in the German Sudeten problem concerns how it came to precipitate Europe into the course of war. Czech ambiguity toward the German minority inhibited the capacity to resolve the problem as an internal one. The protracted negotiations concerning the minority law on the basis of regionalism, decentralization, and proportionalism did not lead to agreement in time. When the initially improving relations between Czechs and Germans were reversed in the thirties, it was too late for a solution within the Czech constitution. The consequences for Czechoslovakia of the economic crisis and of the Nazi rise to power were to make the internal strife both more harsh and more dangerous. German bitterness and antagonism became more difficult to assuage and at the same time Czech intransigence toward an increasingly disloyal minority became more inevitable and justified in Czech eyes. Military contracts were even less likely to go to elements suspected of sabotage, and reclaiming the borderlands through colonization at the expense of the Germans became a matter of vital national security.

When external propaganda stepped in as an additional voice for the German minority, an apparent irredentist situation emerged, escalating toward crisis. In the annexation of the German regions to Germany at Munich there was an apparent crisis solution.

This common perception should be qualified by some historical observations. It must not lead to the erroneous conclusion that the nationalities crisis within Czechoslovakia necessarily led to the solution of Munich, that is, annexation. In the first place, the German minority did not wholly or clearly desire annexation to Germany until the last stages of the crisis. The nationalist Sudeten Deutsche Partei, which since 1936 had garnered two-thirds of the German vote and was the second largest party in Czechoslovakia, did not profess any clearcut aims. It was formed by a combination of extreme Nazis on the one side and moderate autonomists on the other, with all shades in between. The party was mostly in a state of acute internal strife. The leader, Henlein, was genuinely and intentionally all things to all men, single-minded only in building up his power and most likely wanting to assume power in a state of nationalities, to make Czechoslovakia or Bohemia a German-ruled state. In a sense this—making Bohemia German again—was irredentist, just as were Czech attempts to make Bohemia Czech again. There was a certain symmetry here, and when the question became international and the sides were looking for external support, German hopes from Germany were balanced, less successfully, by Czech hopes from their allies, although not all were kinsmen. In fact, the crucial element in the development of the crisis is the extent to which Czech political and military perceptions were dominated and consequently paralyzed by total dependence on concerted action and Allied support. In the end it was not the wishes of the German minority that determined their fate.

Nor was their fate determined by the wishes of the German mother country, which is the second point qualifying the image of a classical irredentist situation. Contrary to mistaken belief, the dismemberment of Czechoslovakia is not at all what Hitler wanted or worked for, although he accepted it in the course of the negotiations for resolving the crisis. There is not a Nazi political or military document on

Czechoslovakia that does not speak of the overthrow or conquest of Czechoslovakia as a whole.[8] The notion of "Bohemia Irredenta" simply does not exist, although the sufferings of the Germans are, of course, loudly proclaimed.

This leads to my third qualifying point, which is that the irredentist character that the Munich settlement assumed was provided by the British, who actively sought to impose a solution that would prevent war, hopefully pacify the Germans, and above all appear moral and just. The term irredentism was not, of course, used. It had a pejorative connotation, probably imprinted on it by bomb throwing in Trieste. Partition—cession of territory, satisfaction of German national aims, justice, and self-determination for the Germans on both sides of the Czech border—seemed the ideal and idealist solution and was therefore widely acclaimed. Even those who suspected that this was not quite what Hitler wanted felt that all the more glory was deserved by those who combined justice and containment in one round.[9]

If we view the isolated case with its set of ethnic conditions, and then view the new map, in which Germans on either side of an international border have become Germans on the same side of the border, we imagine that we have a classic case of irredentism; but in fact irredentism appears more as the temporary consequence of the Munich crisis than as its cause. What the German government wanted was to subvert the Czechoslovak state, what the German minority wanted was to take over the same state, and the solution imposed—apparently so perfectly irredentist—sprang out of the minds of the British as a means to a wider end.

The crisis we call the Munich crisis was not caused by an internal minority problem growing and escalating until it became an international problem. The crisis was caused by the conjuncture of all the central forces in Europe developing since World War I—German foreign policy of revisionism at first and expansionism later, British foreign policy steadily moving toward new alignments in a Europe shaken free of constricting commitments, and the emergence of new problems of nationalities in the successor states. Separate developments converged over the German-Czech problem, which became a means for change for both Germany and Britain. The ethnic and territorial problem was dwarfed by the real issue, which was the state system of Europe. This leads to some reconsideration of the meaning of irredentism.

CONCLUSIONS

Irredentism is an abstract formula that hardly ever fits a concrete historical case perfectly. It is useful as a tool as long as we are not misled into seeing history—or contemporary politics for that matter—in the image of our own theoretical analysis. As an abstraction of real historical phenomena, I suggest that irredentism is a poststate phase of nationalism in which a sovereign power base is in existence, and the energy released by a national movement is directed at some further territorial acquisition or at territorial consolidation, for which there is a case, or a case is made, in terms of historical or religious legitimation.

Seeing irredentism as a stage of nationalism helps us to sort out one of the recurring themes in historical studies of nationalism, namely, value judgments on different types of nationalism. Often we read that certain kinds of nationalism have changed from being liberating, generous forces to become selfish, xenophobic, and aggressive. This personification of change in history is, of course, a mirage in the imaginations of some historians of nationalism. I suggest that such apparent changes are often connected with irredentism in the following sense: the prestate stages of nationalism often concentrate on mobilizing the nation itself through linguistic and cultural activities and persuasion. These activities are regenerative, inward looking, and are viewed by sympathetic outsiders as legitimate and admirable. Once the nation-building process has matured and the sovereign state has been achieved, the arena has to be cleared for political, social, and military activities, and above all that of pursuing a foreign policy. The forces of the national movement, from having been engaged in converting their own battalions, now turn toward the outside world with policies, demands, alliances, and wars. They appear to be fanatically pursuing the fulfillment of further national goals, and often the annexation of further territory.

At such times, when claims invariably clash with those of others and strain the patience of previous supporters, when the leadership has to act from considerations of state policy and at the same time maintain the image of struggling to achieve legitimate aims, we often get the Janus-face of irredentism—self-righteous and self-centered from the inside, arrogant and hypocritical from the outside. To observers who compare it with the previous self-sacrificing nationality, it does seem like a fall from grace.

I claimed at the outset that genuine irredentism springs from an orientation toward a territory more than toward a population, which is often a mere pawn in the irredentist game. Modern irredentism is an outcome of the acceptance of the principle of nationalism, that is, the state in which ethnic, cultural, and political boundaries coincide. Without the principle, cases that do not fit it could not be pointed out. Still, I claim that irredentism as an archetypal force has preceded the nation-state. The principle of the modern nation-state provided the age-long phenomenon of irredentism with its modern rationale and mode of self-expression. Just as patriotism preceded nationalism, as a "natural" sentiment for organized human societies, so irredentism springs from an instinctive, emotional urge. Irredentism, I would go so far as to say, relies on the atavistic "call of the wild" of modern nationalism. It recalls the instinctive urge of humans to define their territory in the same way that animals do, although not by the same physical means. Irredentism brings into play the biological and territorial sources of nationalism, for which it was condemned by the early enemies of the principle of nationalism, such as Lord Acton in the mid-nineteenth century.[10] For Acton, the principle of nationalism meant a regressive coarsening of the fabric of human society toward rule by biological and tribal relationships, and by materialistic and accidental facts. However, the height of human organizational achievement was the intricate structure of a civilized political state, transcending primordial forces and through a perfect architectural design ensuring liberty to individuals and to groups while allowing them to interact and enrich each other's cultures. This idealized confrontation of the ethnic and the pluralistic principles is not irrelevant to the problems of the modern nation-state, but my main reason for mentioning it here is to assert that irredentism is a facet or stage of nationalism that springs from just such an urge as Acton advised to transcend.

Recently there was a debate around a theory elaborated by authors such as Lorenz, Ardrey, and Morris, a group of biological researchers who tried to bring human sentiments, preeminently that of nationalism, as close as possible to biological reactions and in fact drew the above analogy with animals defining territory.[11] Whatever we think of that discredited theory, it is well to remember that irredentism is often a rhetoric that feeds on atavistic feelings for territory and for kith and kin.

Irredentism is hardly ever an automatic sequel to a situation of proximity and ethnic percentages. In the course of history, numerous minorities were either assimilated or remained voluntarily separated from their mother country. Some purposely refrained from carrying the frontier on their back as they migrated. Irredentism begins with a political decision of a state or movement imbued with certain urges and beliefs. One of the classic cases of irredentism is the Jewish claim for Palestine in ancient and in modern times—in both cases a demand for the land irrespective of the wishes of its population. In ancient times, the conquest of the land at God's command was invested with the sublimity of redemption, although the term commonly used is the verb "to inherit."[12] In modern Jewish nationalism, the role of the concept of redeeming the land was paramount, although its practical connotation underwent change. For the first half century of Zionism, redemption of the land was used not only in the new political sense but more in accordance with the biblical sense, to denote, for instance, acres purchased or trees planted or land reclaimed for cultivation.[13] As in other national movements, the time for irredentism proper came as a post-state phenomenon—a combination of an annexationist policy with a belief in a transcendent right to the territory in question. At present we have an irredentist movement completely independent of the existence of an ethnic minority (although that minority is being created).

This last example of irredentism again shows that irredentism is not an outcome of an objective set of conditions but a facet of nationalism with a qualitative set of properties, rooted in certain stages of the historical progression of nations, when the fulfillment of national goals has generated a confidence in the need and right for further territorial objectives.

NOTES

I am grateful to Gal Gerzon for help in locating references.

1. In *Journal of Contemporary History* 14,2 (1979): 287–307.

2. Ibid.

3. K. Hildebrand, *German Foreign Policy from Bismarck to Adenauer* (London: Unwin Hyman, 1989); J. E. Jacob, "Ethnic Mobilization on the Germanic Periphery: The Case of the South Tyrol," *Ethnic Groups* 3, 3 (1981): 253–280.

4. Leo Valiani, "Italia Ed Austria 1866–1915 Nella Storiografia Italiana," *Storia e Politica* 12, 3 (1973): 342–354; E. Maserati, "Un Documento Francese sull' Irredentisimo e la questione Adriatica finite dell' Ottocentro," *Rassegna Storica del Risorgimento* 62, 1 (1975): 63–72.

5. G. Andreopoulos, "State and Irredentism: Some Reflexions on the Case of Greece," *Historical Journal* 24, 4 (1981): 949–959; Paschalis M. Kitromilides, "The Dialectic of Intolerance: Ideological Dimensions of Ethnic Conflict," *Journal of Hellenic Diaspora* (1979): 5–30.

6. E. Benes, *Bohemia's Case for Independence* (New York: Arno Press, 1971; first published in 1917); T. G. Masaryk, *The Making of a State* (New York: H. Fertig, 1969, reprint of 1927 edition); D. Perman, *The Shaping of the Czechoslovak State* (Leiden, 1962).

7. Mamatey and Luza, *A History of the Czechoslovak Republic 1918–1948* (Princeton N.J.: Princeton, University Press, 1973), pp. 26–32; J. W. Bruegel, *Czechoslovakia Before Munich* (Cambridge, 1973), p. 16; E. Benes, *My War Memoirs* (New York, 1928), pp. 451–454.

8. See, for example, *Documents on German Foreign Policy* (Washington, D.C.: U.S. Government Printing Office, 1949), Series D, Vol. II, No. 175, pp. 299–303; No. 259, pp. 420–422; No. 304, p. 504; No. 448, pp. 727–730; Series D, Vol. I, No. 19, pp. 29–39.

9. See, for example, *The Times*, September 7, 1938 and September 9, 1938.

10. Lord Acton, *History of Freedom and Other Essays* (London: Macmillan, 1919), pp. 288–300.

11. See, for example, R. Ardrey, *The Territorial Imperative: A Personal*

Inquiry into the Animal Origins of Property and Nations (New York: Atheneum, 1966).

12. See Genesis XXVIII, 4; Leviticus XX, 24; Numbers XXXIII, 53; Deuteronomy VI, 18; Joshua, I, II.

13. A. D. Gordon, *The Nation and Work* (in Hebrew): *Collected Works* (Jerusalem: Hasifria Hatsionit, 1951), pp. 132–137.

CHAPTER 3

Concealed or Conjured Irredentism: The Case of Alsace

EMANUEL GUTMANN

Meine Leier ist deutsch,
sie klingt von deutschen Gesängen.
Liebend den gallischen Hahn, treu ist
französisch mein Schwert.
Mag es uber den Rhein und über den Wasgau ertönen:
Elsass heisset mein Land; Elsass dir pochet mein Herz.

[My lyre is German,
it chimes with German songs.
Loving the Gallic rooster,
my sword is loyally French.
Let it be sounded across the Rhine and the Vosges:
Alsace is the name of my land;
Alsace my heart beats for you.]

—Daniel Ehrenfried Stoeber (1779–1835)

The war memorial in Strasbourg shows a woman holding in her
arms the bodies of two soldiers, presumably her sons, who had
fought on opposing sides.

By most current theories, irredentism should be rampant in Alsace (the French departments of Haute-Rhin and Bas-Rhin) and in what in France is called Lorraine thioise (the German- or German-dialect–speaking parts of the Moselle department), arguably more so than elsewhere in Europe. This, however, is not the case, nor has it been so at least since the end of World War II, if it ever was an influential movement in that area in the twentieth century. The peak of the irredentist agitation was reached in the late 1920s, after which it declined rapidly, and it came to an end by the events of World War II.[1] In the postwar period, only one such group emerged, and this was more neo-Nazi than irredentist. The Mouvement régionaliste d'Alsace-Lorraine, founded in 1970 by Dr. Iffrig, advocated independence for Alsace and Lorraine within an *"empire européen des peoples germaniques."* This movement never was of much significance and soon disappeared from the scene when major groups split away from it because of its untenable extreme racism.[2] Less radical goals, such as linguistic rights, bilingualism, or cultural or even political autonomy, have often been voiced and continue to be promoted, with little success so far, and they constitute, now as in the past, launchers for the activities of literary and political movements.

What is it that makes these lands—these not-so-peripheral interstices located between France and Germany—the focus of the seemingly gradually diminishing tremors of intra- and intercommunal conflicts stemming from a more than a millennium-old linguistic border? What is it that in spite of the overall tendency causes contradictory, extremist eruptions of an irredentist nature to occur occasionally? Or is the basic containment of this conflict more an appearance than the reality? In any event, recent observations as well as systematic research unmistakably maintain that whatever latent irredentist sentiments may exist in Alsace and Lorraine by far exceed any manifest displays of them. What used to be called *le malaise alsacien* ("the Alsatian malaise") in the interwar period—mainly in France and often in a rather depreciating sense—is nowhere mentioned ever since. The question then arises of the effect of the time factor, in the sense of Alsace continuously being an integral part of France, on the self-identity of the Alsatians and on their particularisms, such as their cultural and linguistic patterns of behavior and the effects of all of these on their political sentiments and stances.

Alsace has been and is a very special "cultural region."[3] Not only is a precise definition of its collective characteristics an almost impossible task for any given moment, over time its identity has undergone constant mutations. In other words, the Alsatian identity is a gradually, and at times not so gradually, evolving lingual tradition. Alsatians claimed in the past (and most do so even today) that the main, if not the only, cultural essence of their region is their language, or their very peculiar language mix. For our purposes here we can ignore the important linguistic fact that the so-called Alsatian dialect is really a mixture of two Germanic languages, the Alemanian and the Franconian, each of which is subdivided in Alsace and Lorraine, and that over and above this lingual parceling almost each village and town had its own lingual peculiarities. The best illustration for this self-conception of the special language as representing the land and its inhabitants is, perhaps, the slogan *"Unsri Sproch isch unsri Seel"* ("our language is our soul"). "There is no Alsatian identity without the dialect," and also "the dialect is the Alsatian identity," wrote Eugène Philipps, perhaps the chief protagonist of contemporary Alsatian cultural particularism. And he added, "The fact of their being French-speaking distinguishes Alsatians from Germans, the fact of their being German-speaking distinguishes them from other Frenchmen, and the fact of their speaking dialect distinguishes Alsatians from both."[4]

René Schickele, prominent writer and pacifist activist of a previous generation, leading exponent of "spiritual Alsatianism" as a major bridge between France and Germany, and after whom the main contemporary Alsatian cultural association is named, tended to emphasize the French element in the Alsatian soul before 1918, when Alsace was under German rule, and stood up strongly for the German element after the return of Alsace and Lorraine to France. In 1918 he said: "Today's Alsatian wants to feel not only as a French citizen; he should learn to love France, without however forgetting Germany, which must mean: to stay true to the German in himself. It would be desirable for France to make use of this situation. In any event, the German element is part of the essence of the Alsatian."[5]

These words were said two generations ago, and although they arguably still represent the feelings and understanding of Alsatians, they leave open a more precise interpretation and they necessitate an attempt to find out what their meaning could be today. There can be little doubt that if Alsace has not already lost its linguistic character of long standing, as some observers claim it has, it is steadily approaching the verge of such a situation. A number of parallel processes are occurring: one is the gradual but steady spread and strengthening of the French language; the other main two are the concurrent decline and decay of the dialects, called by one observer impoverization and bastardization,[6] and retrogression of knowledge of standard German. In other words, what had been, for all intents and purposes, a triglossic situation, in which French had been the H(igh) language, and standard German together with dialect the variant L(ow) languages, is slowly turning into a less complex diglossia with the gradual elimination of standard German. These developments are seeming to accelerate toward the end of this century, notwithstanding the ever-intensifying *Grenzverkehr* (cross-boundary traffic) and the increasing consumption of printed and broadcast mass communication media originating in the neighboring German areas. It should be added, however, that most Alsatian linguistic activists, for what are mainly political reasons, look askance at this differentiation between the two German languages and much prefer to view them as two versions of the same language. But it is precisely this distinction that accentuates the two-pronged but uneven developments of the German linguistic practices.

Because reliable statistics of language use in Alsace do not exist, mainly because such figures are major tools in the incessant struggle over language rights, the following are no more than brief indications of developments. Two hundred years ago, on the eve of the French Revolution and about one hundred years after the French takeover of most Alsatian lands, André Ulrich claimed, "there are three hundred inhabitants of Alsace who do not know French for every one who does."[7] By 1870, the social and administrative elites were said to have spoken French, but in 1918, at the end of the almost fifty-year-long interlude of incorporation in the German Empire, only 2 percent of the population spoke French with any fluency, and only 8 percent more had a relatively good knowledge of it.[8] Thirteen years later, between 50 and 60 percent of the population were able to speak French, mostly as their second (or should one say third) language. From that year (1931) to 1961/1962, the number of people speaking French had increased from 50 to 79 percent in Lower Rhine, from 55 to 83 percent in Upper Rhine, and from 65 to 90 percent in Moselle. Since then, the number of French speakers is approaching 100 percent, most of whom also have reading and writing skills. The number of those knowing only French is increasing, and, what is perhaps of the greatest significance, the number of those for whom French has become their first language has likewise grown considerably. These developments are more noticeable in the larger cities, headed by Strasbourg, and in Moselle.[9]

Concomitant with this persistent gallicanization, the knowledge of German and of dialect is steadily on the decline. Although the overwhelming majority of Alsatians, and a lesser number of Lorrainers, still understand German and speak dialect, all these are rapidly losing ground. Unfortunately, considerably divergent figures to support this phenomenon are being published. By 1964, an estimated 80 percent of Alsatians were unable to write or read German although they spoke their dialects.[10] And it seems safe to say that by the mid-1980s about one-quarter of all Alsatians had little or no knowledge of German at all: some 17 percent could not even understand it and another 8 percent could somehow understand but not speak it. This means that today there exists a somewhat uneven competitive situation between French and the Alsatian dialects, in which standard German has only a minor role to play.

The present-day linguistic problem is not whether the Alsatians possess the necessary lingual competence in order to draw on French sources of their culture, but whether they still possess this same competence in order to draw on the German sources.[11] Or, in other words, a diglossic situation prevails today, which is far from being a regular bilingual order; the attainment, or the restoration, of such an order is what the Alsatian cultural patriots are trying to put on the agenda. They are motivated by the sense that a formal bilingual status is necessary as a rearguard instrument in order to prevent any further retrogression of the dialect and its eventual total evanescence, which would mean the demise of the Alsatian identity. More specifically, the relentless language policy of the French state and particularly the minimal availability of German language instruction in the school system are seen by the Alsatians as direct threats to their language and its dialects. Hence, it is appropriate to view their insistence on a revised language policy for Alsace and/or on augmented and improved teaching of German not as a gesture of obeisance to the Germans and Germany, but as the ways and means to save the Alsatian dialect and its culture and thereby the Alsatian community.[12]

The available evidence suggests that by the early 1990s the intense cultural and organizational efforts of the previous two decades to counteract the general trend of accelerated francization have not been very successful. Whereas before 1968 only one Alsatian cultural organization existed, by 1974 there were eighteen, and even more were set up later.[13] But the number of people actually involved in all these activities seems never to have been more than a handful, and their public impact has throughout remained little more than minimal. Nor have they been able to make appreciable gains in their attempts to get the French state to accept a meaningful bilingual policy for Alsace; moreover, the persistent clamor by small, and in the eyes of the authorities quite unrepresentative, groups for their language rights may have had dilatory effects on them to the extent that they ever had intentions to respond positively to the Alsatian quest.

At the same time, it seems justified to argue that the rather low-keyed literary and linguistic activities that were restarted in the late 1960s and have been continued ever since, even if of late with declining intensity, have been one of the main contributing factors to the gradual displacement of movements and campaigns of a more explicitly political nature. In this connection, it is also of some interest to note that in addition to the more conservative associations, which focus their activities around linguistic problems, there have of late appeared quite a number of more left-oriented groups that are dedicated instead to wider cultural and ecological issues.[14] The main common trend of orientation in recent years seems, however, to have become focused on regionalism, a matter of ever-increasing concern in a number of West European states, and in particular in France.

Without ever having displayed any appreciable interest in regionalism as a general ideology or policy goal, Alsatian leaders have more recently discovered the usefulness of this approach for their particular needs. Being part of a statewide regionalist movement, together with the other linguistic minorities dispersed throughout the six corners of the French hexagon (plus the Corse), has the effect, or at least is considered to have the effect, of mitigating the disagreeableness of having to display unpatriotic pro-German sentiments. It also solidifies a wider front against the entrenched notion of the unilingual character and the intransigent principle of centralism and integrity of the French state. At the same time, the central authorities have always considered regionalism as a policy of deconcentration, actually safeguarding the centralist tendencies or at least as a counterbalance to any extravagant autonomous tendencies.[15]

Of all the French regions, Alsace can arguably lay claim to the greatest degree of regional-cultural uniqueness, if the main indicator for this uniqueness is the regional language, or linguistic situation. Yet even in the case of Alsace this situation cannot be regarded as the sole cause of the regional movement, but rather as a necessary component— at best the single most important one. Regional economic interests and particularly ecological aspirations seek political outlets in a variety of patterns, of which administrative devolution and cultural autonomy seem to be the most commonly agreed within the region.   Other regionalists seek a solution in a supranational or rather suprastate framework, such as in a Contre-les-Etats Europe of Regions or Eth-nies,[16] which would eliminate most present-day one-nation states, and in which Alsace is seen to have the chance to become a region equal to all others. Presently, there are not many takers of this option.

Another idea sees Alsace (and dialect-speaking Lorraine) fused together with adjacent areas to the north and to the east in which Alemanic and Franconian dialects are spoken in a Rhenish entity, sometimes entitled Rhenanie, geographically somewhat similar to the early medieval Lorraine wedged between East and West Francia, and optimistically serving as a bridge between them. Still others foresee for Alsace, or perhaps an enlarged Alsace, with its center at Strasbourg, a future as the capital area of the federated European Community. What all these rather chimerical constructions have in common is detachment from France in varying degrees and modalities, and as such they do not at present find much resonance among the majority of Alsatians. This almost total disowning of all the separatist tendencies and the more radical regionalist inclinations by people who are so strongly attached to their quite unique traditions cannot be explained by simple expedi-ency, but must have potent historical roots as well as definite political orientations based on long experience. In any event, it definitely repudiates any obligatory connection between linguistic-cultural iden-tity and political allegiance.

Alsace is today, and has been for a couple of centuries, peripheral to both France and Germany from a geographical point of view but even more so as far as cultural productivity is concerned, but this has not always been so. The social, cultural, and religious history of Alsace was not just inextricably linked with that of Germany, but for a period of over half a millennium Alsace and its immediately neighboring German lands were at the center of the German world politically and perhaps also economically, and above all by their cultural creativity. Alsace was one of the major seedbeds of the German language and its literature, philosophy, and theology, the German Protestant religion and church.

The incorporation of Alsace into the French state, which started in 1648, was a prolonged process, but by the time it came to its conclusion during the course of the French Revolution many of Alsace's links with Germany were broken off. It was then that Alsace, or the Alsatians, acquired a new identity, which has been changing and redefining itself ever since, but by all counts bilingualism became the central characteristic. German and its dialects remained the spoken language in the home, the street, local business, the church, and also for a long time in the school and in contacts with local authorities. But, on the other hand, French was the language of the Revolution and of personal liberties. Because the persistence of local languages (*les patois*), not only German but many others (more than thirty according to the detailed study undertaken by Abbé Gregoire and reported in 1794), was seen as posing an obstacle to the creation of national solidarity and administrative centralization, the linguistic preponderance of French seemed to be absolutely essential.

This did not mean, of course, the immediate, total assimilation of all minority people, but in the case of the Alsatians, because of their (wrongly) suspected hate for the Revolution and the suspicion of their disloyalty, in 1793 citizens unable to speak French were threatened to be shot, and many were actually executed.[17] Also at that time about 30,000 nobles, Catholic clergymen, and others took refuge across the Rhine. Eighty years later, after the German annexation of Alsace-Lorraine (more accurately, the creation of the administrative province of Elsass-Lothringen), more than 50,000 of its inhabitants, most of them the Francophone minority of Moselle and upper class of Strasbourg, resettled into the French interior. But it was as late as 1853 that French was officially introduced as the language of primary education, and this decree was only very slowly implemented. The overwhelming majority of Alsatians never demanded their reunification with their German cospeakers, and many at the time protested against it, which did not inhibit the authorities of the newly created empire from justifying this annexation by the claim to German soil and fatherland, and the somewhat revolutionary French-ringing Jacobin principle that this fatherland reaches wherever *die deutsche Zunge klingt* ("the German language sounds"). By the way, the only substantial exception from this principle when the new frontier between France and Germany was drawn was the mainly French-speaking area of Metz in Lorraine, which Bismarck's generals convinced him to add to the German territory for military reasons.[18] A few, more minor divergences from the lingual frontier were made in order to annex such areas to Germany, but on the other hand, the French-speaking, and hardly less strategically important, area of the fortress city of Belfort in the southwestern corner of

Haute-Rhin remained French, at least ostensibly because of its unmistakably non-German character.

But other, less cultural and much more power-political arguments have been more prevalent and also more effective on the German (less so the Alsatian) side. Perhaps best-known and representative were Treitschke's often-cited utterances concerning the sacred necessity of German rule over its fatherland, the right of the sword to Alsace-Lorraine, and the Germans' knowing better what is good for the "unfortunate" people of Alsace and the need to "knock sense into their heads."

In the ensuing Franco-German controversy over Alsace-Lorraine, the French side countered the German justifications with two contradictory kinds of arguments. One, which basically adopted the Jacobin principle, was voiced by the historian Jules Michelet, among others, who declared that the Alsatian language was neither proper German nor even a German dialect. The other argument was best expressed by Ernest Renan in his 1882 essay on nationalism, in which he said that neither language nor race and religion offer sufficient foundations for the establishment of a modern nation. Instead, the existence of a nation is a daily plebiscite, that is, the perennially renewed consent and the clearly expressed desire to continue life in common.

However, the fate of Alsace and Lorraine was settled not by such spirited controversies but on the battlefield, but not before the Germans managed, during the years of their rule, to change considerably both the language situation in Alsace as well as the "plebiscitary" national self-identification of many an Alsatian. The Germans reversed in a significant way the previous process of francization and reestablished the ascendancy of the German language and culture to the almost complete elimination of French. They also closely tied the politics and economy of Alsace to those of Germany. But at the same time they seriously alienated many segments of the Alsatian ruling groups, politicians, intellectuals, and others, mainly because of the clumsy handling of the political aspirations of the Alsatians, in particular by their patronizing attitude and the very belated and not quite full conferment of the status of a Reichsland on Alsace-Lorraine. An indication of the divided public opinion on the eve of the war is that although a quarter of a million Alsatians followed their conscription order to the Kaiser's army (of whom more than 30,000 were killed in action), more than 20,000 volunteered to serve in the French army. During all the years of German rule, there were hardly any indications of the existence of a proper irredentist movement. In retrospect, it is difficult to say what the national mood of the population at large really was, and how strong genuine pro-French sentiments were. Nor did the enthusiastic welcome by the Alsatians of the victorious *la belle armée française* as liberators seem to have left much doubt as to their real inclinations and perhaps also their patriotic disposition. In any event, the French, having fought this war as one of revanche, would not even consider deciding the fate of Alsace-Lorraine by a plebiscite, unlike what was done in most of the other German multinational or multilingual border areas.

In the interwar years, especially in the 1920s, with the new and totally reversed political status of Alsace-Lorraine, and given the postwar international atmosphere, *le malaise alsacien* was a virtually unavoidable consequence. The high expectations of the Alsatians for what they conceived as their rights on the one hand, and the French conception of the absolute paramountcy of their one-nation state based on unilingualism on the other, could only lead to an excruciating collision course. To what extent the unmistakably irredentist tendencies and occasional clandestine activities were of a really serious and dangerous nature, as the French nationalists and the government claimed, is difficult to ascertain today. Nor is it possible to do more than speculate where all these activities would have led if they had not been checked rather ruthlessly. There can, however, be little doubt that less extreme movements—some of them just slightly less extreme than the outright irredentists, such as regional autonomists, bilingualists, and other protagonists of language rights—found massive support, although of fluctuating intensity. It also seems quite certain that instigation, and even support, from the outside, such as from Germany, whether governmental or otherwise, contributed to the tense conflictual atmosphere, especially in the mid-1920s, but its overall effect could only have been quite restricted. In the 1930s, with the Nazis in power in Germany, the overwhelming majority of Alsatians were more than hesitant to have anything to do with them, whether for ideological or more pragmatic reasons. In any event, toward the outbreak of World War II these activities had petered out with very few exceptions.[19]

Before that, what brought the situation to the boiling point in the late 1920s more than anything else were the measures that the French government adopted in the returned departments. The uncompromising implementation of the national language policy and the adamant unwillingness to accommodate the Alsatians at least partially must bear the blame for the radicalization of the Alsatian regional activists. The French authorities, or at least some of them, mistrusted the French patriotism of the people of Alsace, even if they did not accuse them outright of pro-German sentiments or worse. Some used the unilingual policy as a continuation of revanchisme by other means. In any event, for many Alsatians the French system was in those years unfavorable when compared with the German as far as civil liberties, including language use, were concerned. The oppressive, and in the eyes of the Alsatians also infamous, language legislation stood out as all the more obnoxious when compared with the government's handling of the religious question.

In June 1924 the Herriot government extended the 1905 legislation separating church from state to Alsace and Lorraine, but after a brief but effective protest movement this measure was withdrawn. This turn of events clearly showed what could be achieved by concerted action, given certain circumstances. In a dialectically interesting way the Alsatians had become more devout Catholics under the Reich and Alsace had become a truly clerical province. Because of the predominantly German-speaking clergy, equally so of the Catholic and Protestant churches, the disestablishment of the churches was clearly seen to constitute a major strike at one of the more powerful Germanophile elements in the land. A renewed attempt by the Blum government in 1936 to modify the constitutional status of the churches in the provinces failed for the same reasons.[20] Since World War II no renewed attempt has been undertaken to equalize the status of the churches in Alsace to that of the rest of the country. In other words, until today this Alsatian legal peculiarity has not been abrogated, which is most astounding for such a highly centralized state as France. What is more, this peculiarity is always adduced as clearly establishing the unique status of Alsace, which would justify other Alsatian peculiarities, and first and foremost those relating to language use.

Whatever links between linguistic and political aspirations might have persisted before World War II, they had to disappear altogether after the war. There had been relatively few cases of clear-cut collaboration during the war; in fact, for most of it, a blatant hostility prevailed between the Germans and the Alsatians, who felt themselves to be under enemy occupation. As a result, any display of what might have been interpreted as pro-German sentiments was out of the question after the war, but not many such sentiments could have persisted in Alsace. At the same time, and for the same very obvious reasons, no German official could make as much as a passing reference to the Alsatian situation in general, and even less so to the language problem. It even took quite a considerable time before serious German scholars were ready to take up research about contemporary Alsatian affairs.

The upshot of all these developments was that since World War II Alsatian political aspirations have been much subdued. Demands for autonomous status or political regionalism have been voiced only intermittently, and more extreme versions have hardly been heard at all. Instead, and also only gradually, calls for bilingualism, and in particular the demand for the promotion of the right to German-language tuition, have become quite popular again.

Right after the war, the teaching of German in the schools of Alsace was totally interdicted, and the public display of German became unacceptable. Given the experience of the Nazi period during the war, no other option was conceivable. This situation, more than anything else, resulted not only in a growing gap between the now outlawed standard German and the dialects that continued to be spoken in the homes and villages, but also in gains of the spoken dialects and the near-displacement of German.

When, in the early 1950s, France slightly relented in its French-only policy, particularly with the 1951 Deixonne Law, which provided for limited study of what were called "local languages and dialects in the regions in which they are in use," three such languages were expressly excluded, namely, Corse, Flemish, and German. The semi-official explanation given at that time was that this continuing exclusion had to be implemented in order "to quell any specter of irredentism on the part of France's former wartime enemies" (!) What this really implied was that these three were considered to be either enemy languages, or *langues allogenes* (languages of other races or peoples). This came very close to branding the people speaking these languages as non-French.

However, although the letter of that law, even where it applied, was most restrictive, its implementation was most uneven and unsystematic. What the law allowed initially was one hour per week of elective study of the regional language in high schools. Only in 1974 was Corsica added to the list of eligible regions, and in 1975 the weekly hours were officially extended to three. But already in 1952, and as a result of considerable local intervention, the teaching of German for three hours a week was reintroduced for children eleven to fourteen years of age.[21] After a 1970 poll revealed that an overwhelming majority of Alsatians were in favor of it, German instruction in the primary schools was gradually introduced in Alsace, starting with the second grade, and it was otherwise augmented as well.

Meanwhile, in the 1960s and 1970s, an escalation of regional cultural and linguistic demands took place in all of France's minority language regions, which gradually radicalized and turned autonomist and even secessionist or irredentist. These awakenings of ethno-national sentiments and even more so the growth of the organizational array in most of these regions as well as in other, French-speaking regions had some repercussions in Alsace, but altogether they did not reach the levels of intensity and politicization in Alsace as they did in the other regions. For one thing, by the 1970s in Alsace the old animosities so prevalent for centuries began to fade away, mainly because the traumas of World War II and all the events leading up to it meant but little to the new generation that had grown up after it. And then, also, this generation was motivated by practical considerations much more than by what were for it atavistic and primordial sensibilities.

Be that as it may, when in the 1980s many regions of minority populations further intensified regional movements—whether based on their cultural and linguistic uniqueness or on other considerations—by and large, Alsace did not. What had actually happened during those years was that ethnic and linguistic groups had benefited by a general tendency to decentralize, which in effect had meant a strengthening of regional subgovernment, or *autogestion* as the French call it. What actually took place, and continues taking place today, is that ethnic sensibilities are being used for other particularistic interests, usually economic, but also for totally different policy goals, including such things as pacificism and ecology. As often as not in these regional endeavors, the strictly cultural elements are being reduced to the level of "symbolic" banners behind which diverse interests join to wage common cause against the centralistic French state.[22] This applies to Alsace as well.

Partly in order to disentangle the narrow cultural concessions, which in any case applied to only a small portion of the territory and population of France, from the much wider, and as a rule more threatening interests, the French government in the early 1980s actually recognized the existence of authentic "regional and minority cultures" for such purposes. Many dozens of "cultural agreements" were signed, which created all sorts of cultural projects in these regions.

However, only a few serious decentralizing measures emerged from such promises of the French government with respect to most of the ethnic regions, and even less was envisaged for Alsace in the first place. At the same time, throughout France, including Alsace, the use of minority languages is in decline, despite the contrary exertions of regional activists, so that its cultural and linguistic unity is not in danger. Moreover, at least as far as Alsace is concerned, the local language protagonists have little room for further expectations in what concerns German language teaching in schools. Moreover, almost nobody of the old established minority groups considers himself as a non-French national; many of them think of themselves as possessing, at best, a dual identity, usually on the basis of bilingualism. This certainly applies to Alsace in the 1980s. Thus the most widespread motto of what is perhaps the leading pro-German group is *Zweisprachig: unsere Zukunft/Notre Avenir est bilingue* ("Our future is bilingual").

As far as Alsace is concerned, the other major factor that had created its unique identity, namely, its special status in religious and church matters and the strong religiosity of its population—which in the past had been expressed in many ways including politically by the vote—is becoming less important because of the steady secularization process taking place even in Alsace.

Internal French developments, including further progress on the route toward regional decentralization and even regional regroupings, do not seem, at this stage, to be in a position to alter the pattern of linguistic trends, to turn back the clock on further linguistic unification, or to upset the strong domestic balances of power that sustain all the processes. Whether exterior developments, and first and foremost those connected with the new political character of a united Western Europe, might detach Alsace from France in one way or another is likewise most doubtful. But, then, the universe of nationalism is as full of surprises as always. Indeed, there is nothing stable or unalterable in these matters in modern times, nor is there anything final about the collective identity and self-definition of ethnic groups over a long period of time. "In a timescale as short as the last sixty years it is difficult to describe the Alsatian identity as anything more than a gradually evolving linguistic tradition, and an associated religious practice, on which feelings of distinctiveness have been anchored."[23] During these years gradual changes have occurred, and there have been as well more abrupt turns of events and profound mutations. Hence it is impossible to say with any degree of firmness not only that outright irredentism and other secessionist goals but even extreme versions of autonomisms have vanished forever. But they seem most unlikely from today's perspective.[24]

NOTES

1. Derek Unwin, "The Price of a Kingdom: Territory, Identity and the Centre-Periphery Dimension in Western Europe," in Y. Mény and V. Wright, eds., *Centre-Periphery Relations in Western Europe* (London: Allen & Unwin, 1985), pp. 151–170.

2. John Loughlin, "Regionalism and Ethnic Nationalism in France," in Y. Mény and V. Wright, eds., *Centre-Periphery Relations in Western Europe* (London: Allen & Unwin, 1985), pp. 207–235.

3. Michael Tocha, "Wesse welle mer, was mer sen gsen," in Rainer S. Elkar, ed., *Europas unruhige Regionen* (Stuttgart: Klett, 1981), pp. 116–126.

4. Eugène Philipps, *Schicksal Elsass Krise einer Kultur und einer Sprache* (Karlsruhe: C. F. Müller, 1980). This is a German translation of *L'Alsace face à son destin. La crise d'identité* (Strasbourg: E. S. de la Basse-Alsace, 1978). It is perhaps of no more than anecdotal interest that Philipps wrote this book in French, and it was translated into German by someone else.

5. René Schickele, *Überwindung der Grenze* (Kehl: Morstadt, 1987), p. 82 (my translation).

6. Meic Stephens, *Linguistic Minorities in Western Europe* (Llandysul: Gomer, 1976), pp. 341–357, at pp. 356–357.

7. Quoted in Stephens, *Linguistic Minorities in Western Europe*, p. 343.

8. Paul Lévy, *La Langue Allemande en France* (Lyon: IAC, 1929), in two volumes; Paul Lévy, *Histoire linguistique d'Alsace et de Lorraine* (Strasbourg: Faculté des Lettres de l'Université de Strasbourg, 1929), also in two volumes; and Malcolm Anderson, "Regional Identity and Political Change: The Case of

Alsace from the Third to the Fifth Republic," *Political Studies* 20, 1 (1972): 17–30.

9. Ludwig Bernauer, "Die Statistik als Spiegel der französischen Assimilationspolitik im Elsass und in Deutschlothringen," in F. H. Riedl, ed., *Humanitas Ethnica. Festschrift für Theodor Veiter* (Wien: Wilhelm Braumüller, 1962), pp. 183–197.

10. Stephens, *Linguistic Minorities in Western Europe*.

11. Jochen Blaschke, ed., *Handbuch der Westeuropäischen Regionalbewegungen* (Frankfurt: Syndicat, 1970); and Heiner Timmermann, "Das Elsass," in H. S. Wehling, ed., *Regionen und Regionalismus in Westeuropa* (Stuttgart: Kohlhammer, 1987), pp. 79–95.

12. Timmermann, ibid.

13. W. R. Beer, *The Unexpected Rebellion: Ethnic Activism in Contemporary France* (New York: New York University Press, 1980).

14. The very insightful article by Solange Gras, "Regionalism and Autonomy in Alsace since 1918," in Stein Rokkan and Derek W. Urwin, eds., *The Politics of Territorial Identity* (London: Sage Publications, 1982), pp. 309–354, seems to have reached different views on some of these matters.

15. Loughlin, "Regionalism and Ethnic Nationalism in France."

16. Alexandre Marc, ed., *Les Regions d'Europe* (Nice: Presses d'Europe, 1973); and Guy Héraud, *L'Europe des Ethnies* (Nice: Presses d'Europe, 1974).

17. Stephens, *Linguistic Minorities in Western Europe*.

18. According to one contemporary, Bismarck actually remarked at the time: ". . . we shall have still more [trouble] with these Lorrainers, who hate us like poison, and will have, very likely, to be roughly handled." H. von Poschinger, *Conversations with Prince Bismarck*, p. 98, cited in C. A. Macartney, *National States and National Minorities* (Oxford: Oxford University Press, 1934), p. 127, fn. 1.

19. Jean-Marie Mayeur, "Elsass, Lothringen und die Deutsche Frage 1870–1945," in J. Becker and A. Hillgruber, eds., *Die Deutsche Frage im 19. und 20. Jahrhundert* (München, 1981), pp. 221–238.

20. Anderson, "Regional Identity and Political Change."

21. Stephens, *Linguistic Minorities in Western Europe*.

22. James E. Jacob and David C. Gordon, "Language Policy in France," in William R. Beer and James E. Jacob, eds., *Language Policy and National Unity* (Totowa, N. J.: Rowman & Allanheld, 1985), pp. 106–133.

23. Anderson, "Regional Identity and Political Change."

24. Raphael Zariski's "Ethnic Extremism among Ethnoterritorial Minorities in Western Europe," in *Comparative Politics* 21, 3 (April 1989): 253–272, is just one recent example of studies of extreme ethnic movements dealing with separatists, secessionists, and irredentists in which Alsace is not so much as mentioned.

CHAPTER 4

Irredentism and Boundary Adjustments in Post–World War I Europe

SHALOM REICHMAN and ARNON GOLAN

Irredentism is a phenomenon that was prevalent mostly in Europe, especially during the first two decades of the twentieth century. It is a particular facet of nationalism, where a national movement that is a minority in a given territory seeks to rejoin the mother country. It therefore has an essentially geographical character, in that it strives to incorporate the territory, and not just its inhabitants, within the boundaries of the mother country. The resolution of irredentist claims was generally achieved—if at all—by the annexation of the territory in question to the mother country.

Irredentism differs both in form and in substance from national movements per se, which seek to attain self-determination in situ and to achieve an independent status as a nation-state. Early in this century, a number of such national movements were very active, striving to break away from multinational empires such as the Austro-Hungarian, the Russian, or the Ottoman. With the breaking up of the multinational empires following World War I, these national movements succeeded in attaining their goals and reached national status within their respective territories, such as Poland, Czechoslovakia, and, to a certain degree, Yugoslavia.

In this chapter we focus on three cases where national phenomena took the form of irredentist claims, that is, where national minorities sought to reunite themselves with the main body of the nation by creating a territorial junction with the mother country. Because of the geographical character of these irredentist claims, they take the form of a territorial conflict, or a special case of boundary adjustments. The minorities in question are all located in proximity to the territory of the mother country, living either in an enclave within another country or in a region with a mixed population, or else the region has been arbitrarily separated from the mother country by an international boundary. In no case was the country hosting the irredentist movement willing to forgo the territory in question, and to settle the conflict—initially—by relinquishing its control over it.

The three boundary conflicts to be discussed are those between (1) Germany and Poland, (2) Italy and Yugoslavia, and (3) Greece and

51

Turkey, all of which have their origins in irredentist claims. Each conflict had a distinct historical background as well as geographical features. Finally, the period selected is that of post–World War I, when the new order in Europe was based not merely on the old ideas of the balance of power but also on the new ideas of self-determination advocated by Wilson in his Fourteen Points. As a result, irredentist claims achieved a recognition of sorts, as legitimate causes for boundary adjustments. More specifically, in addition to the numerous other factors, including strategic, economic, historical, and the like, that were used in boundary delimitations, a new justification for boundary adjustment was recognized, namely, the national aspirations of the population living in the area. This modification was accompanied by a change in the procedure of boundary adjustment, by means of a semi-official hearing procedure where each claimant could present his case.

THE GERMAN IRREDENTIST MOVEMENT IN POLAND

From the late eighteenth century until World War I, the Polish nation was under the rule of three states; two of these, Austro-Hungary and Russia, were multinational empires, and the third was Prussia, whose population was German, and in 1871 served as the unifying factor in the creation of the German Empire. The breaking apart of the two multinational empires enabled the Poles, who were previously ruled by them, to unite and establish an independent state. This process did not occur without struggles with Czechoslovakia and the Soviet Union, neither of whom was, however, as strong as Germany even though it was defeated in World War I. The German army did not lose the war in the east but rather on the western front, and its forces remained in the territory that was part of Germany before the war broke out, such as Prussia, Pomerania, Posen, and Silesia, over which the Poles claimed sovereignty.

The Polish claim was based on two main components, national and economic. The national component relied on the thirteenth of the fourteen Wilsonian principles, the assumption being that anyone who was Polish-speaking belonged to the Polish people and wished to live in a Polish state.[1] Also, under German rule it had been officially established that the criterion of mother tongue should determine nationality.

The second, economic component concerned, specifically, the acquiring of an outlet to the sea. The most accessible location with a safe harbor was the town of Danzig, which was situated at the seaward extremity of the principal maritime route, the Vistula. The problem was that both the town of Danzig and part of the Vistula valley were settled by Germans,[2] especially in the lower part of the region of West

Prussia, Marianwerder. In Germany, there was unwillingness to give up those German regions that had belonged to Germany since before the war, so that in effect the economic and the national problems were closely related.

The Germans put forward a number of practical suggestions to solve the economic problem of providing an outlet to the sea. Thus, it was proposed to turn Danzig, Memel, and Königsberg into free ports and to give the Poles transshipment rights as well as haulage rights to other destinations.[3] The Poles refused these offers, mainly for reasons of national pride.[4]

The Germans relied as well on the Wilsonian principles when they defended their positions at the Paris Conference. They cited, in particular, the principle that called for self-determination for all peoples and for equality and freedom of trade.[5] They brought data showing that there was a German majority in many of the regions claimed by the Poles, such as in upper Silesia, in Posen, and in West and East Prussia. The only areas that the Germans considered as possibilities for annexation by Poland were a number of districts in West Prussia that were populated by a clear majority of Poles, but excluding the city of Danzig, whose population was German. The Germans also asked for a plebiscite in all regions that were candidates to be handed over to Polish sovereignty in order to determine the wishes of the local population, and they suggested exchanges of population in those spots where there were going to remain enclaves and also some compensation for the transferred populations.[6] The Germans argued that if German-settled territories were to be granted to the Polish state, a threat to the security of Europe would be created, because the Germans would strive to regain the territory on which their brethren lived.[7]

As for the economic component, the Germans argued that the severance of upper Silesia from Germany, and in particular the loss of Silesian coal, would cause severe damage to Germany's economy and impair its ability to pay war reparations.[8] The Germans also claimed that the severance of East Prussia from the other regions of Germany (together with the granting of a Polish corridor to the sea) would cause economic ruin to that region due to the increased import costs, because the goods would now have to be transported to East Prussia by maritime instead of overland routes.[9]

Britain, the United States, and France approved the establishment of a Polish state, but there were disagreements among them with respect to both the size and extent of this state. Britain opposed the annexation of territories settled by Germans, including Danzig, to the Polish state because they felt that a relinquishment of many areas would bring about the collapse of the German republic and cause a major problem of

MAP 4.1 Eastern Boundaries of Germany, 1924: Key Map

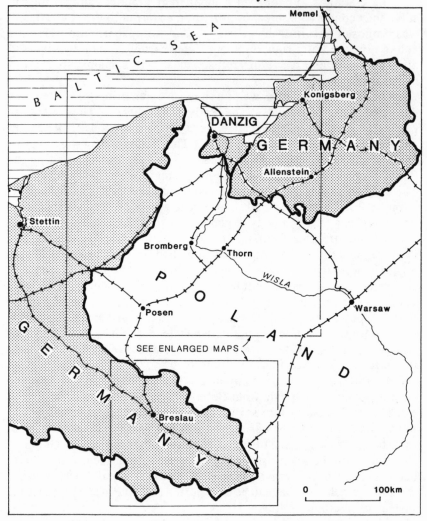

MAP 4.2 **Population and Boundaries in Posen,
West and East Prussia, 1914–1921**

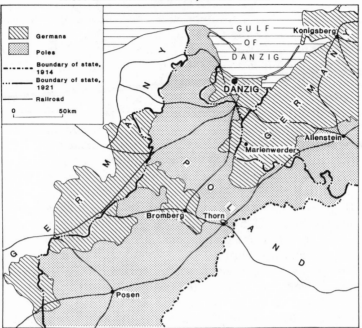

MAP 4.3 **Population and Boundaries in Silesia, 1914–1921**

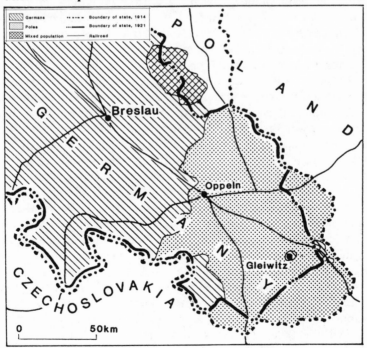

confidence in German public opinion.[10] The United States, on the other hand, was faithful to the principles it had helped to articulate and advocated establishing the frontier on the line that divided the Poles and Germans, while also granting the Poles an outlet to the sea. Geographically this was inconsistent because the valley of the lower Vistula was settled by Germans. The U.S. proposal was hence in the form of a compromise to compensate the Germans for the cutting off of East Prussia by granting them a railway line that would link this region to Germany and would be under German management.[11] The French, however, wanted to weaken Germany as much as possible, and consequently they supported the Polish wishes to receive as much territory as possible at the expense of Germany.[12]

What eventually prevailed was a combination of the British and U.S. approaches, which sought to establish the boundary between Poland and Germany based on ethnic and economic principles, rather than on strategic and political considerations as the French wanted. The solution that was accepted was the transfer to Poland of most of West Prussia and Posen, the territories that contained most of the Polish population under German rule and that also gave Poland access to the sea, and determination by plebiscites in the southern parts of East Prussia and Silesia in which the population would say if it would live in Polish or German territory. In these plebiscites the Poles were defeated, and even in the areas with a substantial Polish majority such as Allenstein and Marienwerder in East Prussia, over 90 percent of the population asked to remain under German rule. This proved the lack of authenticity of the Polish ethnic argument, at least for those areas, as well as for the greater part of Upper Silesia. On the other hand, on the crucial issue of a Polish corridor to the sea and the severance of East Prussia from the territory of Germany, the Poles gained the upper hand. The alternatives that confronted the Paris Conference were either (a) leaving the lower Vistula valley—with its heavy German population—in German hands, and granting free ports and transshipment rights and railway usage to the Poles; or (b) provision of an outlet to the sea to Poland, thereby cutting off East Prussia and leaving a railway link between that territory and the German mainland in German hands. In view of the outcome of the plebiscites, it is doubtful whether the Polish population living in the disputed areas would have objected to remaining in German-controlled territory, had there been a plebiscite on this issue in either Posen or West Prussia. It is clear that in this case the alternative favoring the Polish side was preferred, because Germany was the losing side in the war. Eventually, the outcome was the transfer of more than 1.1 million Germans from the territory of Poland, 900,000 of whom were expelled or left between 1921 and 1931.[13] The rest, together with 200,000 Germans who remained in the Free State of

Danzig, created an active irredentism, striving to reunite with the German state; this became a constant source of tension between Germany and Poland and was one of the causes of the outbreak of World War II in 1939.

ESTABLISHING ITALY'S
BOUNDARY AFTER WORLD WAR I

Italy's emergence as an independent state involved a hard struggle with the Austrian Empire, which ruled the northern part of the peninsula following the arrangements of the Vienna Congress in 1815. The series of wars the Italians waged against the Hapsburg Empire in 1848–1849, 1859, and 1866 resulted in the crystallization of the national territory of Italy. However, the achievements of 1859 and 1866 came to the Italians not through their own military might but rather through the assistance of France (1859) and Prussia (1866). The boundary established after the 1866 war left in the territory under Hapsburgian control two concentrations of Italian population. One was in southern Tyrol, which acted like a wedge between the Italian provinces of Lombardy and Venice. In 1910, 380,000 Italians out of a total of 600,000 inhabitants lived in the Tyrol, according to the Austrian population census of that year.[14] The other concentration was in the province of Kustenland, east of Venice, where 360,000 out of 800,000 inhabitants were Italians, according to the same census.[15]

Among these 740,000 Italians, then, there was a strong irredentist movement, with an objective of reuniting the Tyrol and Kustenland with the Italian state and of separating them from the political system of Austria, in which Italians were second-class subjects of German hegemony. It was a popular movement, not restricted to a social elite.[16] The Italian state, for its part, wished for a reunification of all of this population under Italian rule, as was expressed by Prime Minister Orlando in 1915 when he defined one of Italy's aims in the war as the defense of all the *Genta Italiana*, including those who lived outside the boundaries of the state, meaning also that Italy wished to annex the areas in which these populations lived.[17]

The Italian national movement, however, was not satisfied with the annexation of the areas of irredenta to Italy. Italy had another goal, a strategic one, that would achieve for it the status of a European colonial power akin to France, Britain, and Germany. Therefore, in the agreement to enter the war on the side of the Entente in 1915, Italy demanded, and received in the London Treaty, a boundary line that would pass over ridge lines of the Alps, leaving it with control over mountain passes from Central Europe, and that would include the eastern shore of the Adriatic Sea (Dalmatia) within Italy so that it would have full control

MAP 4.4　The Italian–Yugoslav Dispute

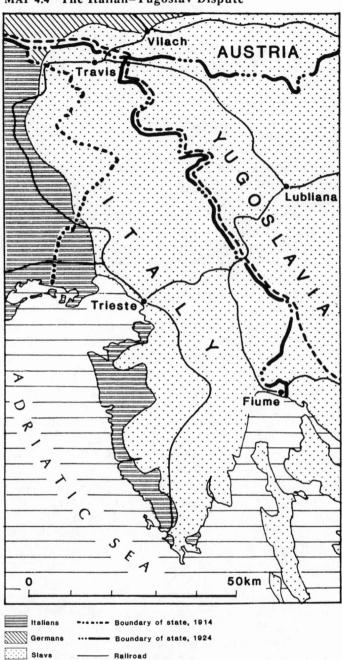

over this sea. This move was intended to enable the Italians to reduce the military forces committed to defend their northeastern boundary and thus enable the splitting up of their forces in their colonies in Libya and the Dodecanese Islands, which they had taken from the Ottoman Empire in 1911, as well as in Eritrea and Somalia.[18] Control of the Adriatic coast, including the ports of Trieste and Fiume of the Austro-Hungarian Empire, would enable Italy to control the imports and exports of the empire because these were the two main outlets to the sea of the entire region; also Italy would profit from the duties and provision of port and shipping services. Thus the Italians hoped to make not only strategic and political but economic gains as well.[19]

The Italian claims also meant, of course, the annexation of about 200,000 Germans in Tyrol and of more than a million Slavs—Slovenians and Croats—in Kustenland and Dalmatia. The Italian claims met the opposition of President Wilson during the negotiations in Paris, because the United States was not a party to the London Treaty and, moreover, Italy's claims contradicted the Wilsonian principles. Instead the United States proposed to Italy a boundary along ethnic lines and the establishment of an independent state in the area of Kustenland and Fiume that would serve as a buffer zone between them, and supported the new Yugoslavian state. The United States also very strongly opposed the annexation of Dalmatia to Italy.[20] Britain also was not enthusiastic about all the conditions of its difficult situation during the spring of 1915, and demanded that Italy make its position more flexible.[21] France was also far from enthusiastic, particularly because it was not eager to see Italy become a major naval power in the Mediterranean.[22] The three Allied powers felt a commitment to the Serbs no less strong than to the Italians, because it was their kingdom that the southern Slavs had incorporated in order to establish Yugoslavia. Also the Serbs, despite the conquest of their country and the subsequent destruction in the war, kept fighting on the side of the Entente in the Macedonian front, and they also wanted to provide Yugoslavia an outlet to the sea. Italy, on the other hand, had caused some disappointment to the Entente when it joined the war, not only because its forces did not cause the expected movement of German forces from the western front, but also because their poor show forced the French and the British to send up forces of their own in order to prevent a military collapse of the Italians.

Regarding southern Tyrol, the powers had less hesitation than about the region that was disputed between Italy and Yugoslavia. The new Austrian republic was too weak to oppose the Italian will—all the more so because as the successor of the Hapsburg Empire it belonged to the losing side in the war. France, which was afraid of an annexation of Austria by Germany, supported, as in the case of the Polish-German dispute, the annexation of territories to Germany's opponents that otherwise were likely to be included in Germany.[23] Britain and the United States, on the other hand, supported the annexation of the regions settled by Italians to Italy, together with areas controlling the routes descending from the watershed line of the Alps southward. In view of the Italian persistence, it was eventually decided to grant the whole of southern Tyrol to the Italians but at the same time to provide the German minority there with minority rights.[24] With this concession the powers hoped to mollify the Italian demands concerning their boundary with Yugoslavia, but this hope was not fulfilled. The negotiations in Paris did not lead to a solution, and the Italian delegation withdrew.

The negotiations on the subject were renewed as direct negotiations between Italy and Yugoslavia, which terminated in November 1920 with the agreement of Rapallo, in which all the province of Kustenland was given to Italy up to the watershed line of the Julian Alps. Fiume was declared an independent city (like Danzig), and Italy withdrew its claims over Dalmatia except the town of Zara (today Zadar), which was left as an Italian enclave.[25] In January 1924, the Italian dictator Mussolini arrived at an agreement with Yugoslavia about the division of Fiume, whereby the city and the port were given to the Italians and all the rest of the area including a side berth of the port and the Slavic suburb of the town were given to Yugoslavia. The agreement included an Italian commitment to help Yugoslavia against any attempt at return by the Hapsburg House and was accompanied by agreements to enlarge the bilateral trade between the two countries.[26] The Italian achievement in this agreement consisted in the fact that the powers that had defended the Yugoslavian interest now tended to move away from the subject. Both France and Britain wanted to see an end to the border dispute in Europe, and they put pressure on Yugoslavia to accept the Italian demands. At the same time, the United States, after Wilson, was becoming more and more isolationist.

The boundaries of the St. Germain agreements with Austria as well as the Rapallo agreement created new problems of irredentism. The Yugoslavian nationalism that opposed the annexation to Italy of regions settled by Slavs was yet in its infancy, and the national movement of the Slovenes and the Croats had been struggling, since the nineteenth century and up to World War I, against other opponents than the Italians. The Slovenes wished for a limited cultural and political autonomy under the Austrian Empire.[27] They were afraid of the holistic Yugoslav framework because, as Catholics with an orientation toward Western Europe, they were not eager to unite with the East European–oriented Greek Orthodox Serbs. A similar problem arose in the case of the Croats as far as unification under Serbian sponsorship was concerned, and they wished to establish a Yugoslavian framework within the Hapsburg Empire that would change the former into a threefold empire in which the Germans, Hungarians, and Yugoslavs would have equal status.[28] The opponents of the southern Slavs on the national issue within the empire were the Germans and the Hungarians, who wanted to leave the status quo, in which they were superior to the Slavs, intact. The Slavs had less friction with the Italians because the latter were also in an inferior status vis-à-vis the Germans and Hungarians.[29] But with World War I and the Italian claims, the main opponent of Yugoslav nationalism became Italy, and the struggle with Italy became a joint interest of the Croats, Slovenes, and Serbs. However, this Yugoslav unity was accompanied by many internal conflicts, which eventually weakened the joint struggle on the establishment of the boundary with Italy.[30]

With the inclusion of Fiume and the provinces of Kustenland and southern Tyrol in Italy's territory, the Italians promised that they would uphold the rights of the German minority; however, they did not stand by their promise and, beginning in 1921, implemented a policy of settling Italians from southern Italy in the German areas of southern Tyrol.[31] This process was much accelerated by Mussolini's accession to power. In the agreement of Rapallo, the Slavic minority was promised that their national rights would be safeguarded, they would receive cultural autonomy, and their communal institutions and national language would be respected. But in Mussolini's regime the Slavic minority rights were not honored and, what is more, pro-Yugoslav propaganda was prohibited and strict censorship was applied to the press and to Slavic literature.[32] This is how the process of "exchange of irredenta" came about: the Italian irredenta under Austrian rule gave way to Austrian-German and Slavic irredenta under Italian rule. Italy, for its part, aimed to create an Italian empire, and for that purpose tried to dominate territories settled by foreign peoples that were important for strategic and economic reasons, while at the same time trying to suppress the national feelings of these peoples.

The Italians considered themselves as one of the Entente powers that had won the war, and after the London agreement they did not see any reason to justify their demand for territories on the basis of self-determination in the same way as the Austrians and Yugoslavs did. The thrust of their argument was political and strategic, although Wilson's fierce opposition to any demand that went beyond ethnic lines forced them to adduce arguments with a national and ethnic base. The Italians argued that the Slavs in the region spoke Italian, their way of life was Italian, and those who opposed integration between Slavs and Italians were newcomers there.[33]

TURKEY AND GREECE:
THE ERADICATION OF IRREDENTA

The Ottoman Empire ruled over the Balkans and Asia Minor from the fourteenth and fifteenth centuries until the end of the eighteenth century, with scarcely any disturbance. During this period the Greek population, scattered in these areas, was also under its rule. The ideas inspired by the French Revolution, however, which began to penetrate the area toward the end of the eighteenth century, included aspirations of breaking the Ottoman yoke and the renovation of Greek independence.[34]

The core of Greek nationalism was situated at the western coast of Asia Minor, in the cities of Izmir and Istanbul, where lived the Greek elite, mostly rich merchants and officials in the Ottoman administration. In European Greece, most of the Greek population consisted of poor peasants subject to Ottoman feudal lords. The low socioeconomic condition of the Greeks in Europe drove them, and not their brothers in Asia Minor, to rise against the Ottoman Empire in 1821.[35] The motivation of the people was nationalistic, and the local leaders wished to replace the Ottoman landlords.[36] The area of the Greek state established in 1829 was small—the Peloponnisos peninsula, Attica, and the zone north to the Gulf of Corinth; most of the areas populated by Greeks remained under Ottoman rule. This situation was far from satisfactory to the Greek nationalists, who aspired to the materialization of the Megali Idea—the reunification of all Greeks living in the Balkan peninsula and Asia Minor within the framework of a Greek state. But the existence of an independent Greek state encouraged the irredentist movement in the areas that did not come under Greek sovereignty, a movement that now strove for unification with the Greek state.[37]

The enlargement of the Greek state was gradual and piecemeal. Honoring the coronation of the new king, in 1863 the British donated the Ionian Islands to Greece; in 1881, as a consequence of the Berlin Congress, Greece won Thessaly at the expense of the Ottoman Empire. This slow pace of territorial expansion did not satisfy the many nationalistic Greeks who lived within the borders of the Ottoman Empire, and many of them migrated into the Greek state. There they tended to agitate the Greek society and to strengthen the aspiration for the fulfillment of the Megali Idea.[38]

Even the optimists among the Greeks did not believe that the Ottoman Empire would easily give up its capital city and main ports, Istanbul and Izmir, to Greece. It is important to note that in the same period other Greeks, mainly from the Aegean Islands (then under Ottoman rule) and most of them poor farmers and fishermen, emigrated to Asia Minor where they found their living as small merchants and farmers in the new villages erected along the new railways then built by the Ottoman government.[39]

The inability of Greece to defeat the Ottoman Empire was manifested in 1898, when the Greek army attempted the conquest of Macedonia and Crete and were defeated by the Ottomans. This showed that the only way to win a war against the Ottoman Empire was through a coalition of the Christian Balkan states. Such a coalition was indeed assembled to defeat the empire in the first Balkan war (1912–1913), and forced it to concede almost all of its European territories. But another result was that Greece had to accept the fact that a considerable part of the territory included in the Megali Idea, areas in Macedonia and Thrace, passed into Serbian and Bulgarian hands. Greece had to be satisfied with southern Macedonia and most of the Aegean Islands— still quite a remarkable gain. About a quarter of a million Greeks, excluding the population of the conquered territories, were added to the population of Greece as a result of an immigration wave from the Ottoman Empire after the Balkan wars.[40] An agreement of population exchange, 200,000 from each side, was concluded between Greece and the Ottoman Empire in 1914 because of this wave, but it was not carried out because of the outbreak of World War I.[41]

MAP 4.5   Population Around the Aegean Sea, 1912

At the end of that war, the Ottoman Empire collapsed and the European powers divided its territory among themselves. Greece, as a junior partner in the Entente, saw it as an opportunity to fulfill the Megali Idea, and under the leadership of Prime Minister Venizelos the Greeks invaded Asia Minor (May 1919), took over Izmir and its vicinity, and conquered Thrace up to the gates of Istanbul. In the peace treaty signed with the Ottoman Empire in Sèvres in August 1920, Thrace was granted to Greece and Izmir remained in Greek hands as a mandate.[42]

The Turkish national movement, which emerged after the defeat, did not accept the treaty of Sèvres. Led by Mustafa Kemal, it opened a military struggle against the Entente forces stationed on Asia Minor's soil. Greece offered to repress the newborn Turkish national movement, but was defeated (1920–1922). The Greek army left Asia Minor, and most of the Greek population there, about a million people, followed it, propelled by a massacre committed by the Turks against the Greek and Armenian population of Izmir. Shortly after, they were followed by 300,000 Greek inhabitants of eastern Thrace who were deported by the Turks. In the Lausanne agreement that officially ended the Turkish-Greek war (1923), the deportation of the Greek population was placed within the framework of a wider population exchange, as half a million Muslims were sent from Greece to the new Turkish republic.

Thus the Greek attempt to fulfill the Megali Idea in its territorial aspect failed, although as a consequence of the Lausanne agreement almost all Greeks of Asia Minor and Thrace came under Greek rule. This was the end of a process that had begun almost one hundred years before when Greece attained independence, an end marked by the eradication of irredenta through migration and population exchange. There was almost no territorial change between the 1913 and 1923 boundaries of Turkey and Greece in Asia Minor and Thrace (Greece having gained western Thrace from Bulgaria). What did change was the distribution of Greek and Turkish populations. Despite the nationalistic character of the conflict, when it came to the determination of whether an individual was Greek or Turkish, the only criterion was the old Ottoman miliet, the religious group. In order to distinguish between a Greek and a Turk in several zones of Anatolia and Thrace it was necessary to know a person's religion, because after hundreds of years of living together Greeks in those areas spoke Turkish and lived a Turkish way of life, and were distinguishable from their Turkish neighbors only in their religion (which proscribed intermarriage).[43]

SUMMARY AND CONCLUSIONS

The irredentist problem resulted from the spatial distribution of European peoples, which left national groups under alien rule and aspiring for unification with their homelands. This problem was one of the reasons for the outbreak of World War I, as it caused tensions in the relations of the Hapsburg Empire with Italy and Serbia, and between Greece and Turkey. With the end of the war this problem was brought to the center of the political arena. President Wilson in his Fourteen Points and Prime Minister Lloyd George (although for less idealistic reasons) understood the importance of avoiding its re-creation as a consequence of the peace treaties. But they could not withstand the demands and pressures of their allies such as France (in the Polish case), Italy, and Greece, and thus new irredenta were inevitably created for national, strategic, political, and economic reasons.

In the Polish-German case, economic needs, such as having an outlet to the sea, and strategic considerations, such as the need to keep Germany from getting too strong, resulted in the creation of a German irredenta in the "Polish corridor" and adjacent areas under Polish rule. In the Italian case, it was possible to demarcate a reasonable ethnic boundary line between Italy, Austria, and Yugoslavia, but the Italian aspirations to rule the Adriatic Basin and become a first-rank colonial power necessitated strategic boundaries along different lines. Thus, although the Italian irredenta was united with Italy, two new irredenta were created, consisting of German and Slavic people. In the third case, the Greeks had a national interest in controlling the northern and western shores of the Aegean Sea and its islands as a continuation of the century-old process of shaking off the Ottoman yoke and uniting the Greek people under Greece's sovereignty. The collapse of the Ottoman Empire after World War I seemed to the Greeks an opportunity to fulfill their national goal, but an underestimation of the newborn Turkish national movement, as well as loss of the support of the Entente powers, prevented its realization. As a result Greeks were deported from the Turkish republic, a process completed with the population exchange between Greece and Turkey. Thus, the solution to the Greek irredenta involved no territorial exchange.

Differing methods, then, were employed to solve the irredenta problems of the period in question, ranging all the way from population exchange or deportation on the one hand to the assurance of minority rights on the other. It turned out that an agreement of population exchange proved the most stable: it included compensation and reha-bilitation of the populations involved, and succeeded in lessening friction between two alien ethnic groups and rival states. On the other hand, compromise measures did not work, and solutions such as assur-ing minority rights and economic interests and the establishment of independent city-states like Danzig and Fiume retaining a mixed popu-lation, were unsuccessful. In the nationalistic atmosphere of countries like Italy, Germany, and Poland between the two world wars, irredenta were a source of permanent friction and tension between old and newly created states, and eventually were an important factor in bringing Europe to World War II. It appears that these lessons were not lost on the powers who reshaped the boundaries of Europe after World War II: thus Poland was moved westward and all its German population was forced to relocate within the boundaries of the two new German states, without leaving any German minority in Poland. The Italian-Yugoslav boundary was redemarcated according to ethnic lines, thus leaving most of old Kustenland in Yugoslav hands at Italy's expense. As in the Greek-Turkish case, the solution was total, forced by the victorious side on defeated Germany and Italy; and as of today, more than forty years later, those arrangements seem stable.

The irredenta problem is a component in the framework of boundary disputes; other components are economic, strategic, historical, and attitudinal.[44] Territory is a framework for a state's potency, a part of its heritage, a source of its pride. Territory is also associated with human and economic resources: recruiting soldiers, natural resources, and so on. By possessing a certain territory a state can gain an advantage by denying its resources to a rival state, as the Italians did when they prevented Yugoslavia from using the ports of Trieste and Fiume.

The importance of an irredenta problem differs according to the differences between boundary disputes. Whereas in the Italian-Yugoslav dispute the irredenta problem was minor, in the two other cases it was central. The intensity of the irredenta problem and its role in a boundary dispute were greater according to the magnitude of the differences between the different national groups and the majority of the population, or between two national groups. Thus there was a deep cleavage between Protestant Germans and Catholic Poles, or between Muslims and Greek Orthodox.

A final point concerns the procedure of solving, or managing, an irredentist or a territorial conflict. From the Paris conference in 1919 onward, conflicts of this nature were brought before a quasi-judicial tribunal, which judged the case on its merits. In some cases this tribunal enacted certain fairly universal rules or principles, which were more or less binding on the parties. This procedure also had an effect on the stability of the territorial conflict.

NOTES

1. H. W. V. Temperley, *A History of the Peace Conference in Paris*, Vol. 6 (London: H. Frowde, 1924), pp. 235–236.

2. Ibid., p. 258.

3. *The German Counter Proposals to the Paris Peace Conference* (Berlin, 1919), pp. 46–47.

4. P. Mantoux, *Paris Peace Conference, 1919* (Geneva: Librairie Droz, 1964), p. 157.

5. *German Counter Proposals*, p. 31.

6. Ibid., pp. 32, 42–49.

7. Ibid., p. 44.

8. F. Czernin, *Versailles, 1919* (New York: H. P. Putnam's Sons, 1964), p. 342.

9. R. Donald, *The Polish Corridor and the Consequences* (London: T. Butterworth, 1929), pp. 78–82.

10. Czernin, *Versailles*, p. 210.

11. H. I. Nelson, *Land and Power: British and Allied Policy on Germany's Frontiers 1916–1919* (London: Routledge & Kegan Paul, 1963), pp. 148–149, 153–154.

12. N. J. G. Pounds, *Poland Between East and West* (Princeton: D. van Nostrand, 1964), p. 63.

13. R. Hartshorne, "Survey of the Boundary Problem of Europe," in C. C. Colby, ed., *Geographic Aspects of International Relations* (Port Washington, N. Y.: Kennikat Press, 1970), pp. 175–176; G. Labuda, *The Territorial, Ethnical and Demographic Aspects of Polish-German Relations in the Past* (Poznan: Instytut Zachodni, 1962), p. 30; R. Machray, *The Polish-German Problem* (London: George Allen & Unwin, 1941), p. 44.

14. R. Albrecht-Carrie, *Italy at the Paris Peace Conference* (New York: Anchor Books, 1963), p. 373.

15. A. E. Moodie, *The Italo-Yugoslav Boundary* (London: G. Philip & Son, 1945), p. 147.

16. O. Jaszi, *The Dissolution of the Habsburg Monarchy* (Chicago: University of Chicago Press, 1929), p. 395.

17. Albrecht-Carrie, *Italy*, p. 45.

18. Ibid., pp. 372–375.

19. Moodie, *Italo-Yugoslav Boundary*, p. 171.

20. Albrecht-Carrie, *Italy*, pp. 191–193, 364–366.

21. Mantoux, *Paris Peace Conference*, p. 192.

22. Albrecht-Carrie, *Italy*, p. 113.

23. Ibid., p. 424.

24. Ibid., pp. 419–422.

25. Moodie, *Italo-Yugoslav Boundary*, pp. 173–176.

26. Ibid., pp. 203–207.

27. B. C. Novak, *Trieste 1941–1954* (Chicago: University of Chicago Press, 1970), pp. 17–18.

28. C. Rogel, "The Slovenes and Yugoslavism 1890–1914," *East European Quarterly* (1977): 102–103.

29. Novak, *Trieste*, pp. 8–9.

30. I. J. Lederer, *Yugoslavia at the Paris Peace Conference* (New Haven: Yale University Press, 1963), p. 83.

31. M. Toscano, *Alto-Adige, South Tyrol* (Baltimore: Johns Hopkins University Press, 1975), p. 11.

32. Lederer, *Yugoslavia*, p. 165.

33. O. Marinelli, "The Regions of Mixed Population in Northern Italy," *Geographical Review* 2 (1919): 135–138.

34. S. G. Chaconas, *Admanitos Korais: A Study in Greek Nationalism* (New York, 1942), pp. 28–31, 35–37.

35. C. M. Woodhouse, *A Short History of Greece* (New York: Praeger, 1986), pp. 114–118.

36. Ibid., pp. 128–130.

37. Ibid., p. 156.

38. G. Augustinos, *Consciousness in History* (New York: Columbia University Press, 1977), pp. 18–19.

39. A. J. Toynbee, *The Western Question in Greece and Turkey* (London: Constable, 1923), pp. 123–127.

40. A. A. Pallis, "Racial Migrations in the Balkans, 1912–1924," *Geographical Journal* 66 (1925): 317–320.

41. J. Hope-Simpson, *The Refugee Problem* (London: Oxford University Press, 1939), p. 15.

42. P. C. Helmreich, *From Paris to Sevres* (Columbus: Ohio State University Press, 1974).

43. Hope-Simpson, *Refugee Problem*, pp. 14–15.

44. In the years preceding World War I and during the war and the Paris peace conference, problems of boundary making raised a great deal of interest among geographers. Part of the contemporaneous literature on the subject of boundary includes: A. P. Brigham, "Principles in the Determination of Boundaries," *Geographical Review* 7 (1919): 201–219; Curzon, Lord of Kendlestone, *Frontiers* (Oxford, 1907); J. Cuijic, "The Geographical Distribution of the Balkan People," *Geographical Review* 5 (1918): 345–361; R. Hartshorne, "A Survey of the Boundary Problems of Europe," in C. C. Colby, ed., *Geographical Aspects of International Relations* (Port Washington, N. Y.: Kennikat Press, 1970); C. C. Hyde, "Notes on Rivers as Boundaries," *American Journal of International Law* 6 (1912): 901–909; D. W. Johnson, "The Role of Political Boundaries," *Geographical Review* 4 (1917): 208–213; L. W. Lyde, "Types of Political Frontiers in Europe," *The Geographical Journal*, 45 (1915): 126–145; M. I. Newbigin, "Race and Nationality," *The Geographical Journal* 50 (1917): 313–335; J. Pratsch, "The Geographical Conditions of National Defence," *The Journal of Geography* 13 (1914-1915): 102–110; and S. N. Patten, "The Unnatural Boundaries of European States," *The Survey* 34 (1915): 24–27, 31–32.

CHAPTER 5

Irredentism in Germany Since 1945

RICHARD STOESS

At first sight, Germany appears to be a rewarding object of study in irredentism. Apart from the National Socialist "Greater German Reich," which existed only during World War II, there was always a considerable discrepancy between ethnic and political borders.

The German people have traditionally lived in different states. Until the middle of the nineteenth century, a variety of small states was the rule. In 1871, the German Reich, founded under Prussian hegemony, represented a "small German solution" (*kleindeutsche Lösung*) because Austria was excluded.

After World War I, Germany lost

- North Schleswig to Denmark
- Eupen and Malmedy to Belgium
- Alsace-Lorraine to France
- West Prussia, Posen, parts of East Prussia, Outer Pomerania, and Upper Silesia to Poland
- The Memel region, first to the Allies, then to Lithuania

In addition, the Saar district was mandated to the League of Nations and Danzig was declared a free city. Also Germany was forbidden to unite with Austria, which had itself lost South Tyrol, South Styria, and the Sudetenland.

After World War II, all regions east of the Oder-Neisse line were lost: East Pomerania, East Brandenburg, and Lower and Upper Silesia, as well as the southern part of East Prussia to Poland and the northern part of East Prussia to the Soviet Union. The Saarland was given political autonomy, but was economically under the control of France.

This article was prepared for publication in December 1986. In 1990, the FRG and the GDR were united and the Order-Neisse border recognized by the German government. Expelee organizations, however, do not accept the loss of the former eastern territories beyond this border. And among German minorities in Poland, the Soviet Union, Czechoslovakia, and Romania, irredentist feelings are growing. Thus in the future Germany may indeed become a rewarding object of study in irredentism.

From 1939 to 1945, eighteen million Germans lived in the areas east of the Oder and Neisse, including some who lived in other East European countries. Between 1945 and 1982, some nine million German expellees from former eastern territories of the Reich as well as three million refugees from the Soviet-occupied zone (German Democratic Republic) fled to the western zones (Federal Republic of Germany). In 1976, about four million Germans were presumed to be living in East European countries. An estimate of their distribution was as follows:

Soviet Union	1.8-2,000,000
Poland	750,000
Romania	400,000
Hungary	300,000
Czechoslovakia	100,000
Yugoslavia	12,000

Yet despite the discrepancy between political and ethnic boundaries, irredentist cleavages never dominated German political history to the extent that many people believe. This misconception is almost certainly due to the Nazi exploitation of irredentist feelings to justify their own expansionist policy, which was based on spurious notions of Germanic racial identity.

Hitler's expansionist, imperialist, and racist policy, and the Pan-Germanic and folkish goals of the Nazis, had nothing to do with the real claims of German minorities in other countries. German fascism was founded on ideological patterns: antiliberalism, anticommunism, and national socialism. *Lebensraum* ("living space") or *Volksgemeinschaft* ("folkish community") are terms known only in the German language.

An examination of the period after 1945 shows how little influence irredentism proper exerted, despite the large losses of territory Germany had to accept after the war started by the Nazis was finally lost. Only three irredentist issues were of some importance after World War II: the Danish minority in Schleswig-Holstein; the Saar conflict; and the expellees and German minorities in Eastern Europe. It should also be noted that after World War II, the people of Alsace no longer felt any considerable identity with Germany. Therefore, there was no objection among the population to the region being returned to France and no resistance to the French policy of assimilation. Since the late 1960s, however, there has been a growing regional movement within the "Dreyeckland" (the triangular land area between France, West Germany, and Switzerland). But this is in no way an irredentist movement; it is concerned with the cultural identity and self-determination of the whole region as well as environmental issues.

THE DANISH MINORITY IN SCHLESWIG-HOLSTEIN

After the wars between Germany and Denmark (1864) and Germany and Austria (1866), the duchy of Schleswig was incorporated into the new Prussian province of Schleswig-Holstein (1867) and then into the German Reich (1871). In 1920, North Schleswig, as the result of a referendum, was returned to Denmark whereas Middle Schleswig voted for German status (hardly any Danes lived in South Schleswig). Approximately 50,000 Danes live in the Federal Republic of Germany (FRG) today.

Demands by the Danish minority for a revision of the German-Danish border after 1945 failed because of the attitude of both the British occupying authorities and the Danish government. In order to gain a license for their own party, the South Schleswig Voters League (SSW), the German Danes restricted their claims in 1948 to political and cultural autonomy: South Schleswig, they maintained, should be separated from Holstein and have the status of a special province within the British-occupied zone. But even this goal became anachronistic after the consolidation of the FRG and was dropped. The SSW has changed in the last thirty years from a separatist national party to a minority and regional party that represents the social and cultural interests of Danes in Schleswig-Holstein. In addition to ethnic consciousness, the party promotes the ideals of tolerance and understanding between European peoples.

This change is related to the economic and social integration of the Danish minority and also to their success regarding their own cultural policy. For example, there are fifty-five schools and sixty-three kindergartens in Schleswig that are administered by the Danish school board but paid for by the Schleswig-Holstein provincial government.

The extent of the integration of the Danish minority is expressed by the fortunes of the SSW in regional elections. In 1947, it obtained 99,500 votes (9.3 percent) and six representatives. In 1983, it received only 21,000 votes (1.3 percent) and one representative.

THE SAAR CONFLICT

The Saar district was separated from Germany by the Treaty of Versailles (1919) and placed under the mandate of the League of Nations. France received the coal mines and the right to exploit them. In 1925, the Saarland was incorporated into the French customs area. The French interest in weakening Germany's military and industrial potential, however, found only limited support among the Western powers. France was indeed able to occupy the Rhineland, but the attempt to separate the area east of the Rhine failed because of opposition by the

United States and Great Britain. Even the future of the Saarland was to be determined after fifteen years by a referendum. This took place in 1935 and led to the reincorporation of the Saarland into the German Reich.

In 1945, the Saarland (whose population numbered about a million) was first occupied by the United States but taken over by the French in July of that year. In 1946, France separated the Saarland from its zone of occupation, then annexed it to its economic and customs area and gave it the status of political autonomy. France secured its political and economic influence in two ways: the constitution of the Saarland (1947) affirmed the status quo, and (with the exception of the Communists) only pro-French parties were allowed. The first provincial elections (1947) were regarded as a test of the constitution. The strongest party became the Christian Peoples party (CVP), with about 52 percent of the votes; the next strongest was the Social Democratic party of the Saarland (SPS), with almost 33 percent. Both parties formed the government under Prime Minister Johannes Hoffmann (CVP), who ruled until 1955.

The pro-German opposition to the situation of the Saarland as a state that, if not annexed by France, was still dependent on it, developed both in West Germany and the Saarland itself. The FRG government and the German parliament never tired of confirming the status of the Saarland as a German province. However, the foreign policy of Chancellor Konrad Adenauer always avoided undertaking anything that would interfere with the process of Franco-German reconciliation and European unity. Opposition was stronger, however, in the West German parties, particularly the Liberals and Social Democrats, and also in extraparliamentary politics (e.g., the German Saar League).

Inside the Saarland itself, all opposition to the pro-French course was suppressed. Only the Communist party of the Saar (KPS) could officially criticize the government, but for reasons of ideology and program it did not represent an electoral alternative for most Saarlanders. Dissatisfaction with the policy of separation could be expressed only in two ways: by withholding votes or spoiling ballot papers, or by building pro-German factions inside the parties loyal to the system. The second alternative was the only one that presented a chance of long-term success, as the Hoffmann government could always argue that the majority of Saarlanders supported its policy.

Pro-German factions developed in all the loyal parties. They were weakest in the Christian Peoples party and strongest in the Liberals, where in 1950 a pro-German group was even able to take over the leadership. As a result the Democratic party of the Saar (DPS) was outlawed in 1951, and thus became the focal point for opposition in the Saarland until 1955.

With the integration in the west and the rearmament of the Federal Republic of Germany, a solution to the Saar question had to be found. The Federal Republic and France agreed to a "Europeanizing" of the Saarland within the framework of the West European Union. However, this solution depended on a referendum. Preparatory to the referendum, pro-German parties (CDU, SPD, DPS) were permitted, which joined together to form the Heimatbund (Home League). In 1955, almost 68 percent of Saarlanders voted against this Europeanizing. The Hoffmann government resigned, and in 1957 the Saarland was incorporated in the Federal Republic of Germany as the tenth Bundesland. The Social Democratic party of the Saarland integrated with the SPD, the Christian Peoples party (except for a small minority) with the CDU, and the Democratic party of the Saar became the regional branch of the Liberal Free Democratic party (FDP).

EXPELLEES AND GERMAN MINORITIES IN EASTERN EUROPE

The territory of the Federal Republic of Germany represents only 53 percent of the territory of the Third Reich, and the German Democratic Republic (GDR) only 23 percent. The remaining 24 percent, that is, about a quarter of the old Reich (described as "former eastern territories"), belongs today primarily to Poland and the Soviet Union.

Approximately a fifth of the population of the Federal Republic consists of East European expellees and refugees from the German Democratic Republic. However, some four million Germans still live east of the Oder-Neisse border.

The phenomenon of the expellees was not always a result of forced expulsions. Many inhabitants of the former eastern territories and Russian-occupied zone fled from the Red Army or were, for economic or political reasons, not prepared to live under a socialist regime.

The official position of the Federal Republic of Germany on these matters is complicated. The Federal Republic regards itself as the legal successor of the German Reich (that legally still exists within the borders of 1937) until a peace treaty with the four powers of the anti-Hitler coalition clarifies the German questions in terms of international law. In this context the Federal Republic does not regard the German Democratic Republic as a foreign country, but it respects the border between the FRG and the GDR and the Oder-Neisse border between the GDR and Poland subject to a future peace treaty and rejects the use of force as a means of revision of international borders. The problem of expellees is therefore not primarily a question of irredentism. As far as the problem of expellees concerns their integration into West German society, it is mainly an economic and social one. And as far as it concerns their claim to a "home in the east" (*Heimatrecht im Osten*), it is a national question, namely, the question of the reunification of Germany.

However, the division of Germany has produced problems with an irredentist component. Many German minorities live in East European countries. They strive for recognition as ethnic minorities with their own cultural identity (German lessons in schools, FRG school books, magazines, libraries, radio and films, and so on). This is strongly supported by the FRG government through international agreements. In addition, the reunification of families in the Federal Republic is encouraged. However, the extent of cultural autonomy is regarded by concerned groups as quite inadequate, and it can be assumed that the situation would be even less satisfying without the efforts of the FRG government. With the passing of generations and the continuous resettlement of Germans from the east, the problem of the actual ethnic minorities will probably be of decreasing importance in the future.

A further and more important irredentist component of the problem of the division of Germany is created by the attitude within those groups in West Germany who feel themselves to be minorities, acting accordingly and expecting to be treated accordingly. In their view they are representatives of the former Eastern German population or of the German minorities still living in East European countries. They have combined together into cultural associations (*Landsmannschaften*). This "proxirepresentation," or self-claimed right of representation, has been very important in the history of the Federal Republic of Germany.

The structure of organization of expellees in the Federal Republic was, from the beginning, of an ambivalent character. In order to promote their economic and social interests expellees founded pressure groups and political parties so as to have immediate access to political power. The all-German Bloc of Expellees and Victims of Injustice was active between 1950 and 1960 and was represented in the FRG government as well as in different provincial and local governments. Its successor organization is the All-German party, which still exists but since 1966 has had no parliamentary representation. The pressure groups have been particularly successful in influencing all political parties on the issue of the "equalization of burdens" legislation (*Lastenausgleich*), as a consequence of which 150 billion DM have been distributed to expellees up to this time.

The cultural associations, on the other hand, maintain an attachment to their old home and promote cultural traditions. Whereas the political parties and pressure groups are losing importance because of the increasing integration of expellees into the FRG economic and social system, the demand for "right of abode" in the east is still very strong in the cultural associations (expellee status is passed on to the children of the original expellees). The League of Expellees (*Bund der Vertriebenen*) allegedly has two million members. It incorporates twenty-one cultural associations including the Sudeten-German cultural association (maximum membership 350,000) and the cultural association of Silesia (maximum membership 150,000). The cultural associations of East Prussia as well as that of Pomerania are smaller but very active groups. Expellee associations constitute an important political basis for criticism of the status quo in Central Europe. They are not prepared to accept the existing borders and oppose every policy that would mean an easing of relations with the East. Also they demand the return of the "stolen territories," as the former eastern territories are referred to by such groups. Their claims are in excess of those for reunification. For the leaders of the expellees it is always a question of their "folkish" identity. They see themselves as displaced national minorities, as people from Danzig, as Carpathian Germans or Danube Swabians who have been driven from their rightful home.

THE ISSUES OF IRREDENTISM IN GERMANY

Irredentist demands are normally formulated by the ethnic minorities themselves. The FRG government is very restrained with respect to these problems. It limits itself to demands, within the framework of international negotiations, for the guarantee of the rights of minorities and for self-determination. Even in the case of Saarland Germans, the government did not behave otherwise, although the population of the Saar was against the status of autonomy and would vote for reincorporation within the Federal Republic. The policy of the FRG government in the 1950s was to promote integration in the west, equality with partner states, and agreement with noncommunist neighbors. There was no interest in the revision of borders in the west or the north. Also, the national question was thought to be solvable only with the agreement of European states.

Although eastern expellee groups put forward irredentist claims, they are not an ethnic minority in the strict sense of the term. However, they organize themselves according to ethnic principles and maintain their local customs and historical traditions, while trying to keep their regional consciousness alive and strive for the repossession of their original homelands.

The typical forms of organization for the realizing of irredentist demands in Germany are the party or the association. Their traditional target of appeal is the state. In Germany social movements as a form of organization are rare, although elements of such movements can be found among the expellees.

Organizations include only part of those concerned. In the Saarland there was, for a time, a pro-French majority among the Germans, not least because the association with France brought with it considerable economic and social advantages. Organizations of Danish minorities in the immediate postwar years were popular even among the non-Danish population because Denmark generously distributed food parcels (*Speck-Dänen*). As things got back to normal the number of German Danes involved in organizations declined, as was the case with expellees in general. At no time did the expellee parties receive more than half their potential votes, and 20 percent is the highest percentage of expellees organized in associations at any one time.

Irredentist demands in Germany are also aimed at border revision. This was only realistic, however, in the case of the Saarland, because France could produce no historical or ethnic justification for the separation of this region. With the Franco-German reconciliation, European unity, and the military integration in the West, a solution for this problem had to be found. And so the pro-German opposition was fighting for a goal that was very likely to be achieved. This was not the case regarding the question of the German-Danish border. At first the British occupying powers prevented any modification of the border, which later became unrealistic with the establishment of the Federal Republic of Germany as a sovereign state within the European Community. The Danish minority found no support for their aims, not even from the government of their mother country; so instead they concentrated on gaining cultural and political agreements that made their existence as an ethnic minority more comfortable.

This was also valid for the expellees. If one ignores the spectacular verbal revanchism of some expellee functionaries, then demands of the eastern expellees are always mainly concerned with their "right to live in the west" (*Lebensrecht im Westen*), that is, their social, economic, and cultural integration into West German society. The expellees have achieved this goal thanks to the incomparable willingness of the indigenous population to share their own prosperity. Even though it would be wrong to see the chauvinism expressed during some conventions of the expellees as harmless, one should also avoid exaggerating its importance. The fact of being an expellee and the consciousness of being a minority are continuously losing their power to influence the behavior of expellees, and the readiness to return will probably decrease as time goes on.

In the pursuit of irredentist goals, legality is always preferred, and actions are within the framework of the system. Extraparliamentary opposition, unconventional participation, or violence hardly ever appear. Even in the Saarland, where the pro-German opposition was often suppressed with questionable methods, there was no appearance of illegal forms of resistance. Furthermore, this also obtains for expellees, who now have their representatives in all parts of the political system. One exception was their opposition to the new eastern policy of the FRG chancellor Willy Brandt at the beginning of the 1970s.

CONCLUSION

In looking at the situation in West Germany after 1945, the first question that arises is why the dissatisfaction with the division of Germany was not greater. In view of the many millions of expellees who sought refuge in the almost totally destroyed "west zones," the Allies feared social problems of major dimensions. There was thought to be the danger of a new form of class struggle between the indigenous population and the expellees and refugees who needed food, accommodation, and work that were not available in the west zones, even for their own residents. The enormous loss of territory and the occupation by Allied troops could have produced another wave of disruptive German nationalism. After all, the consequences of the Treaty of Versailles were still remembered.

But none of this came about. Overall, the development of the Federal Republic of Germany up to the late 1950s was a perfect example of economic prosperity and political stability. The reasons for this apparent anomaly were essentially political, with both external and internal dimensions.

Because of the East-West conflict and the iron curtain, which ran through the middle of Germany, there was no realistic alternative to integration into the West. In political fringe groups there was some consideration of the neutrality issue, possibly on the Austrian pattern, which might have led to unity. But the expellees and Christian conservative citizens, who tended to be particularly nationalistic and anticommunist, rejected a neutral Germany because they thought that it would be defenseless against communism. It was particularly West German nationalism that for considerations of both ideology and security accepted the division of Germany and tolerated, if not compelled, integration into the West. And this meant the recognition of the Western borders. As for the East, there have, of course, been enormous reservations. But this did not lead to internal conflicts because the policies of the West German state were not the object of criticism. It led instead to militant anticommunism, which was directed as much at Socialists and Communists in the Federal Republic as against the GDR and the Eastern bloc.

This consensus in foreign policy was extended during the 1950s to include an internal political consensus concerning important economic and social issues. By the end of the 1950s there was a basic consensus encouraged by the effects of the economic miracle, which precluded any real success for fundamental opposition to the FRG government. Only three parties were represented in the FRG parliament, and their programs and policies could be differentiated no longer in terms of substance but only in terms of details.

This exceptional capacity for integration is not necessarily of a lasting nature. The possibility cannot be ignored that economic and political crises could revitalize the national question and, with it, irredentist claims. At present, however, the basic consensus does not seem to be in danger.

REFERENCES

Jochen Blaschke, ed., *Handbuch der westeuropaischen Regional-bewegungen* (Frankfurt am Main, 1980).
G. Robert Boynton and Gerhard Loewenberg, "The Development of Public Support for Parliament in Germany 1951–1959," *British Journal of Political Science* 3 (1973): 169–189.
Jane Perry Clark Carey, "Political Organization of the Refugees and Expellees in West Germany," *Political Science Quarterly* 66, 2: 191–215.
David P. Conradt, "Changing German Political Culture," in Gabriel A. Almond and Sidney Verba, eds., *The Civic Culture Revisited* (Boston/Toronto, 1980), pp. 212–272.
Walter Randall Craddock, "The Saar-Problem in Franco-German Relations 1945–1957," Diss., Ann Arbor, 1961.
Frank Dingel, "Die Christliche Volkspartei des Saarlandes; Die Demokratische Partei Saar; Die Kommunistische Partei Saar; Die Sozialdemokratische Partei des Saarlandes," in Richard Stoess, ed., *Parteien-Handbuch*, vol. 1 (Opladen, 1983), pp. 719–806; and vol. 2 (Opladen, 1984), pp. 1852–1879, 2217–2240.
Bundesminister des Inneren, ed., *Eingliederung der Vertriebenen, Fluechtlinge und Kriegsgeschaedigten in der Bundesrepublik Deutschland* (Bonn, 1982).
Jacques Freymond, *Die Saar 1945–1955* (Muenchen, 1961).
Imanuel Geiss, "Die Rechtsopposition und ihr Kampf gegen die Ostvertraege," Schriftenreihe des "Pressedienst der Demokratischen Aktion," no. 9, Muenchen n.d.
Rudolf Grulich and Peter Pulte, eds., *Nationale Minderheiten in Europa* (Opladen, 1975).
Johannes Hoffmann, *Das Ziel war Europa* (Muenchen/Wien, 1963).
Eberhard Jaeckel, ed., *Die Schleswig-Frage seit 1945. Dokumente zur Rechtsstellung der Minderheiten beiderseits der deutsch-daenischen Grenze*, Frankfurt am Main/Berlin 1959.
Hiddo M. Jolles, *Zur Soziologie der Heimatvertriebenen und Fluechtlinge* (Koeln/Berlin, 1965).
Raning Krueger, "Entstehung, Entwicklung und Wandel des Suedschleswigschen Waehlerverbandes (SSW) 1945–1983," master's thesis, Freie Universitaet Berlin, Fachbereich Politische Wissenschaft, Berlin, 1984 (mimeo).
Ruprecht Kurzrock, *Minderheiten* (Berlin, 1974).
Wilfried Lagler, *Die Minderheitenpolitik der schleswig-holsteinischen Landesregierung waehrend des Kabinetts v. Hassel (1954–1963)* (Neumuenster, 1982).

Peter Paul Nahm, *Doch das Leben ging weiter. Skizzen zur Lage, Haltung und Leistung der Vertriebenen, Fluechtlinge und Eingesessenen nach der Stunde Null* (Koeln/Berlin, 1971).

Franz Neumann, *Der Block der Heimatvertriebenen und Entrechteten 1950-1960* (Meisenheim am Glan, 1968).

Karl-Friedrich Nonnenbroich, "Die daenische Minderheit in Schleswig-Holstein nach 1945 unter besonderer Beruecksichtigung des Suedschleswigschen Waehlerverbandes," Diss., Kiel, 1972.

Robert H. Schmidt, *Saarpolitik 1945-1957*, 3 vols. (Berlin, 1959-1962).

Dieter Marc Schneider, "Saarpolitik und Exil 1933-1955," in *Vierteljahreshefte fuer Zeitgeschichte*, vol. 25 (1977), no. 4, pp. 467-545.

Heinrich Schneider, *Das Wunder an der Saar. Ein Erfolg politischer Gemeinsamkeit* (Stuttgart-Degerloch, 1974).

Richard Stoess, "Der Gesamtdeutsche Block/BHE; Die Gesamtdeutsche Partei," in Richard Stoess ed., *Parteien-Handbuch*, vol. 2 (Opladen, 1984), pp. 1424-1477.

Kurt P. Tauber, *Beyond Eagle and Swastika. German Nationalism Since 1945*, 2 vols. (Middletown, 1977).

Vertriebenenpolitik heute, ed. by the Hanns-Seidel-Stiftung. Akademie fuer Politik und Zeitgeschehen, Schriftenreihe no. 12/13, Muenchen, n.d.

Gerhard Ziemer, *Deutscher Exodus. Vertreibung und Eingliederung von 15 Millionen Ostdeutschen* (Stuttgart, 1973).

CHAPTER 6

The Ups and Downs of Irredentism: The Case of Turkey

JACOB M. LANDAU

According to a document I discovered in Istanbul[1] (to be published elsewhere), the Ottoman Sultan Mahmut I issued an important imperial order on December 20, 1745, commanding cavalry officers to ready their troops to proceed to Kars for a war against Persia. The reasons given for the decision to fight Persia were as follows: (1) to defend the true faith from heresy; (2) to protect the Ottoman Empire from the evil designs of Persia's ruler, Nadir Shah; and (3) to redeem Azerbayjan. Although the redeeming of Azerbayjan was only third on the list, following the religious and military arguments, it is noteworthy. Not surprisingly, Azerbayjan had been part of the Ottoman Empire, and the majority of its inhabitants spoke Turkish (as they still do). Although Mahmut I could hardly have reasoned in irredentist terms 240 years ago (if he had, he would probably have argued that the Azerbayjanis were Turks!), one may perceive the seeds of future irredentist thinking in the Ottoman Empire and the Republic of Turkey insofar as redeeming territories was concerned.

I would tentatively define irredentism as "an ideological or organizational expression of passionate interest in the well-being of an ethnic or cultural minority living outside the boundaries of the states inhabited by the same group." However, moderate expressions of interest or defending a group from discrimination or assimilation may not be irredentist phenomena at all; hence a more adequate definition of irredentism may be "extreme expressions, ideological or organizational, aiming at joining or uniting (i.e., annexing) territories that the ethnic or cultural minority group inhabits or has inhabited at some historical date." Nevertheless, one ought also to accord brief attention to the moderate expressions (for example, in the cultural domain), as they may well lead to the extreme ones. This is certainly true of the Turkish case and applies to several others as well.

This chapter is a brief exposé of Turkish irredentism, highlighting its main stages and characteristics and enabling, perhaps, profitable comparison with other types of irredentism prevailing elsewhere. With the exception of a perceptive article by Myron Weiner,[2] such comparisons seem rarely to have been attempted.

First, we shall consider the preparatory stage: in our case, developments among the Tatars in Czarist Russia, one of the Turkic groups that, as part of a cultural revival in the late nineteenth century, became increasingly aware of common historical and linguistic ties with other Turkic groups and most particularly with the Turks in the Ottoman Empire. To comprehend the nature of this revival properly, one should realize that it was largely a response to the official Czarist policy of Russification, often accompanied by Christianization, during the latter part of the nineteenth century. This policy, intensified by Izvolsky's support of Pan-Slavism, provoked the minority groups in the Czarist empire, of which the Turkic groups numbered 13,600,000 out of a total population of 125,600,000 (about 10.82 percent), according to the 1897 census. The response of these Turkic groups, which extended over vast territories, could be expressed within two parameters—religious and nationalist. Islam (later Pan-Islam) came first and was more easily understood by the masses as a unifying bond against external dangers. Turkism (later Pan-Turkism) was adopted as a bond by some members of the elite soon afterward. This chapter is concerned with the latter phenomenon alone.

The Tatars had been under Russian domination longer than any Turkic group; by the late nineteenth century they were heavily subjected to the pressures of Russification.[3] The Crimean Tatars, in particular, were surrounded by non-Turks, and their only chance for national survival lay in the development of relations with other Turkic groups, particularly those in the relatively nearby Ottoman Empire. An active bourgeoisie arose, rivaling its Russian counterparts in business[4] and capable of initiating and leading a cultural revival. The key figure in this revival was Ismail Gasprinsky (1851–1914)—also known by his Turkish name, Gaspirali—who was most active in education, journalism, and language reform. In 1884, as mayor of the Tatar town of Bahçesaray, he devised a new school curriculum for the six-year local schools, introducing (among other reforms) the Turkish language as well as the previously taught Arabic. By 1883, he had already founded a newspaper, too, the *Tercüman* ("Interpreter"), in which he advocated secular nationalism with a definite Pan-Turk cultural inclination. Having attained a circulation of 5,000 in the 1880s and 6,000 in the early 1900s[5] (quite an achievement for that time), *Tercüman* increasingly preached union of all Turkish people in Russia, thus arousing the suspicions of the Okhrana, the Russian secret police.[6]

Gasprinsky also devised a lingua franca for Turkish groups in Russia and abroad. Well aware that the main differences among the Turkish languages and dialects were not variations in syntax or accidence but rather in vocabulary, Gasprinsky strove to "purify" this new language of foreign words, employed only in certain areas, substituting others of

Turkish or Turkic origins and comprehensible to the elites (a parallel effort attempted, somewhat less successfully, to minimize phonological diversity). The result was a language easily understood by Turks in the Ottoman Empire, including Tatars.[7] Schools in Bahçesaray taught this language and *Tercüman* propagated it elsewhere. The theme of language reform was soon taken up by local newspapers in Azerbayjan and Bukhara as well. This was of some significance, as no fewer than 250 newspapers (some ephemeral indeed) were published by Turkic groups between 1905 and 1917.[8]

Although it is difficult, if not impossible, to evaluate Gasprinsky's impact precisely,[9] one may safely say that despite its primarily cultural nature, it laid the groundwork for political Pan-Turkism of an irredentist character. Political demands with clear Pan-Turk leanings predominated at the three all-Muslim congresses that met at Nidzhni-Novgorod in August 1905, St. Petersburg in January 1906, and near Nidzhni-Novgorod in August 1906. Representatives of Turkic groups—especially those of the Tatars—were in a definite majority at all three congresses.[10] Subsequently, in 1907, Ali Hüseyinzade (1864–1941), a Caucasus Tatar, defined the objectives of Turkic nationalism in his journal *Füyuzat* ("Enlightenment") as "Turkism, Islamism, and Europeanism," with the first value considered as the most important.[11] Another Tatar, Yusuf Akçura, or Akçuraoğlu (1870–1935), was even more explicit: in his journal *Kazan Muhbiri* ("The Kazan Correspondent"), published since 1906, he expressed deep commitment to the Pan-Turk cause. In 1904, he had determined the bases for political Pan-Turkism in a long article prudently printed abroad in the Cairo newspaper *Türk*. The article, entitled "Üç tarz-i siyaset" ("Three Systems of Government"), and later issued as a pamphlet, lauded Turkism as the only realistic means of effecting a national union of all Turks, with Turkey at its center.[12] For the first time, Pan-Turkism was preached as a political doctrine and was suggested as the only viable category of nationalism capable of saving the Ottoman Empire. Irredentism had come into its own as the central political element in the Pan-Turk ideology.

Antigovernment agitation by Turkic groups in Czarist Russia during World War I, their various revolts, and their continued resistance to Soviet rule during the first decade of the new regime have been variously interpreted by Soviet, Turkish, and other analysts; most agree about the nationalist Pan-Turk character of all this.[13] However, active Pan-Turkism was subsequently relegated to isolated cases alone, after the Soviets pitted minority groups against one another and set up allegedly autonomous subdistricts emphasizing the small ethnocultural subdivisions among the Turkic groups.[14] The center of Pan-Turk political activity had moved, even during World War I, to the Ottoman

Empire, where its irredentist character soon became prominent.

THE FLOURISHING OF
IRREDENTISM IN THE OTTOMAN EMPIRE

The propagation of Pan-Turkism in the late Ottoman Empire was largely due, on the one hand, to the activity of Tatar intellectuals who had immigrated from Russia and, on the other hand, to the writings of several Ottoman thinkers. Its penetration of small but influential elitist circles was due in no small degree to the political fortunes and intellectual makeup of the empire.[15]

Immediately before and during World War I, leading Tatars like Hüseyinzade and Akçura and prominent Azeri journalists such as Ahmet Agayev (Agaoğlu) (1860–1939), all of whom had displayed marked interest in Pan-Turkism, left Russia and settled in Istanbul. There, they contributed their share to the public debate on the nature and fortunes of Turkish nationalism. Prominent among the Ottoman intellectuals then busily engaged in the debate were Ziya Gökalp and Tekin Alp. Although neither was a Turk (the first was a Kurd, the second a Jew), both played a key role in the formation of early twentieth-century nationalist thinking among Ottoman Turks. Ziya Gökalp (1876–1924), although a prolific writer,[16] exerted an impact on Pan-Turkism only via a few poems and articles and several pages of his last book. Nevertheless, he may be credited with systematizing Turkish thinking on Pan-Turkism and using his immense prestige to encourage its consideration and acceptance as a point of departure for public debate. Among his poems, "Turan," written in 1911, refers to a huge, undefined land in Central Asia, the common birthplace of all Turkic groups. It was an unequivocal call for an irredentist Pan-Turkism: "For the Turks, Fatherland means neither Turkey, nor Turkestan, Fatherland is a large and eternal country—Turan!" When World War I broke out, Gökalp composed another fiery poem, "Kizil Destan" ("Red Epic"), calling in no uncertain Pan-Turk terms for the destruction of Russia and the liberation of Turks there. The impact of Gökalp's poems on the Turkish population was far-reaching, but his articles had a more lasting influence on several intellectuals. Using the sociological tools of the day (Gökalp was himself a lecturer in sociology at Istanbul University), Gökalp examined the meaning of the concept of nation. Defining it in cultural terms, he concluded that the Turkish nation had three circles: the Turks in Turkey; the Turkmens in Azerbayjan, Iran, and Khwarizm; and the more distant Turkic-speaking peoples in Central Asia (Turan). The first were united, the second would be at some future date, and union with the third was envisioned for the distant future. This was a three-stage political program for irredentists, with debate centering not on the aims but only on the timing and methods.[17]

Tekin Alp (1883–1961) was less well known but nonetheless highly influential. Born as Moïse Cohen at Serres, in Macedonia, he lived in Salonica until 1912. There he met Gökalp, who left an indelible impression on the younger Tekin Alp. He then moved to Istanbul and became a major advocate of irredentist Pan-Turkism, as reflected in his newspaper articles and books. Two of his most outstanding works were published in the fateful year 1914. The first, in Turkish, was entitled *What Can the Turks Gain in This War?*; it was translated a year later into German as *Türkismus und Pantürkismus*.[18] In it he argued that the new Turkish nationalism, or Turkism, could be equated with its strongest component, Pan-Turkism. He called on the movement to become as irredentist as its Italian or Romanian counterparts and wished it as large a measure of success. This appears to be the first explicit public appeal in the Ottoman Empire for an irredentist, politically minded Pan-Turkism.

Tekin Alp elaborated this theme in another Turkish book, a lengthy essay on the Pan-Turk ideology, focusing on the happy lands of Turan. Assuming that Turks had common origins, history, language, traditions, customs, social institutions, literature, and sentiments, he maintained that Turan was a living reality of 10,800,000 square kilometers and 43,000,000 Turks, many of them governed by Russia and China, against whom the thrust of this work is aimed. For winning Turan, Tekin Alp formulated maximum and minimum plans resembling those of Gökalp and called on Turks everywhere to unite against Russia and China in order to establish a large "Golden Fatherland" with Istanbul as its capital.[19]

The works of Gökalp and Tekin Alp were merely the most prominent of a spate of books, pamphlets, and newspaper articles, all of which sought definitions of the Turkish identity and emerged with irredentist formulas applicable to the salvation of the hard-pressed Ottoman Empire. The greatest success of these Pan-Turk circles, highly vocal but small in numbers, was the adoption of the Pan-Turk ideology by several top political leaders; in fact, Pan-Turkism, with its irredentist overtones, became the official ideology of the Ottoman Empire for a while. In 1908, the Young Turks revolted against Sultan Abdülhamid II, and a year later they deposed him. In effect, they ruled the empire for a decade, until its defeat and dismemberment in 1918. At first, they had substituted their own Ottomanist views for Abdülhamid's Pan-Islamic ideology, enjoining on all inhabitants to exert a joint effort to save the hard-pressed empire. But the separatist movements continued to gather momentum, some with their own irredentist character (Greek, Montenegrin, and Romanian, for example). Consequently, the increasingly desperate quest for identity impelled its ruling elites to search for another solution to save the empire. Pan-Turkism was the obvious choice; although Pan-Islam and Ottomanism were not entirely abandoned, some government officials and many intellectuals indeed opted for Pan-Turkism.[20] Various popular organizations in Istanbul and elsewhere supported the ideas of Turkish nationalism, such as the Türk Ocaği ("Turkish Hearths"), established in 1911, which dispatched trusted members during World War I to recruit support abroad for Pan-Turkism.[21]

Although the Committee of Union and Progress, as the organization of the Young Turks was called, placed considerable emphasis on the Turkification of language, education, and business, some of its attention was devoted to absorbing immigrant Turks for provinces lost in the Balkan wars and organizing those remaining there to cement their ties with the Ottoman Empire. Pan-Turk sentiment increased in the committee, particularly after Ali Hüseyinzade, who had migrated to Turkey, joined the committee's Central Council in 1911.[22] Pan-Turk propaganda campaigns were conducted by the committee's agents in Azerbayjan, the Caucasus, Turkestan, Iran, and Afghanistan, as well as among the Volga Tatars.[23] The main proponent of the committee's Pan-Turk policies was Enver, who became minister of war. The Ottoman Empire's declaration of war in 1914 included the following phrases: "The ideal of our nation and our people leads us to the destruction of our Muscovite enemy, obtaining thereby a natural frontier for our Empire, which should include and unite all branches of our race."[24] The commitment to Pan-Turkism explains the undertaking of the abortive Ottoman offensive in the Caucasus in late 1914 and early 1915, the strong-handed exile of the Armenians some time later (as they were considered a barrier to Pan-Turk unity), the transfer in 1917 and 1918 of units badly needed on the Syrian and Mesopotamian fronts for a thrust into southern Russia up to Baku, and, obviously, the intense Pan-Turk propaganda throughout the war. Last, Enver himself, dreaming of a Turkish-Turkic state even after the Ottoman Empire's defeat, turned up in Central Asia in 1921 and raised the banners of Pan-Turkism and Pan-Islam against the Soviets, only to die there in battle a year later.[25]

THE FORTUNES OF
IRREDENTISM IN THE REPUBLIC OF TURKEY

Thus ended the Pan-Turk plan of the Young Turks; but the dream lived on, nourished by irredentist dreams. However, since irredentism appears to require full-scale war as the only feasible means of changing frontiers, Pan-Turkism had to lie low during peacetime. Among the

Turkic groups abroad, it appeared to die a natural death under such authoritarian regimes as that of the Soviet Union and to lead a precarious existence in such countries as Cyprus and Romania or among émigrés in Western and Central Europe. Turkey itself, however, was to be the key to the survival of the movement and the ideology it fostered. Constituted as a republic and impelled by its founder and president, Mustafa Kemal, toward speedy modernization[26] and Westernization, the new state and its leadership had little if any use for Pan-Turkism. Well aware that Pan-Turkism's irredentist factor could endanger the new republic's relations with the Soviet Union, Mustafa Kemal drove this ideology to the periphery of public life. Instead, he promoted his own brand of nonirredentist nationalism, focusing on Turkey itself. The glorifying of the Turks' ancient past was stripped, indeed, of its political content and presented in strictly cultural and social terms—as the official state ideology of the republic.

Latent Pan-Turkism lingered on, however, throughout the 1920s and 1930s (Kemal died in 1938). Irredentist sentiment found expression in several pamphlets and periodicals published by small Pan-Turk groups. These journals were generally short-lived, primarily because official censorship closed them down in Turkey and banned the import of similarly minded works published in Europe by Turkic émigrés from the Soviet Union. In Turkey itself, immigrants set up their own separate *Landsmannschaften*, each with its own bulletin promoting the particular brand of irredentism espoused—evidently focused on the *Diş Türkler* ("Outside Turks") in their country of origin. Such particularist attitudes only served to foster the divisiveness that further enfeebled the Pan-Turk movement in Turkey between the world wars. The movement became noticeable, although still small in numbers and restricted in activity, only after several local Turks joined in the 1930s. Its best-known exponent was Hüseyin Nihal Atsiz.

Atsiz (1905–1975),[27] a schoolteacher, journalist, and novelist, devoted most of his adult life to organizing and leading the Pan-Turk movement in the Republic of Turkey; together with his brother, Nejdet Sançar (1910–1975), he worked on reshaping its ideology in an even more irredentist direction than before. Atsiz set up a clandestine association, and in 1931–1932 was the first to publish and edit a Pan-Turk periodical in the Republic of Turkey, followed by another in 1933–1934. Initially, these generally resembled other Pan-Turk publications, writing and commenting on the history, language, literature, and present circumstances of Turkic peoples. Soon, however, the periodicals assumed a more militant stance, not only in their strong anticommunist propaganda line but also in their attempt to preach Pan-Turkism as contrasted with "Anatolianism" (a semiderogatory term by which they referred to Mustafa Kemal's Turkey-centered brand of nationalism). A distinct trait was added to Pan-Turk ideology by Atsiz, Sançar, and several others of the same persuasion: racism. Although the cultural and geographical perspectives were not abandoned, the Pan-Turkism of the 1930s emphasized the racial bond. As its exponents phrased it, blood was the best and possibly the sole meaningful bond of the Turkish race,[28] a great and superb one, surpassing all others.[29] Consequently, the minorities in the Republic of Turkey were not part of the Turkish nation, whereas the "Outside Turks" were. Ideologically, Atsiz would label himself "a racist and a Pan-Turkist"; he considered himself a popular leader and even affected some of Hitler's mannerisms.

World War II witnessed a resurgence of irredentist sentiment in the Republic of Turkey. Extreme Pan-Turks, although still modest in overall number, considerably intensified the content and tone of their propaganda—in direct proportion to their hopes for a radical change in the status quo of the "Turkish world." Turkey's situation in World War II was basically different from conditions prevailing in World War I. A large empire no more, the Republic of Turkey remained neutral until February 22, 1945, shortly before the war ended. Its government proclaimed martial law and insisted on strict maintenance of its neutral stand. This, however, mattered little to Pan-Turks. Their irredentist hopes for the downfall of the Soviet Union and the consequent "liberation" of the "Outside Turks" were fanned by the German advance since June 1941. Pan-Turks in Turkey then believed in and increasingly preached the approaching defeat and dismemberment of the Soviet Union. Their journalistic activity focused on convincing Turkey's president, Ismet Inönü, to enter the war: "O Inönü, selected by history for this great day! We are ready to shed our blood for the sacred independence of Turkdom! All Turkdom is anticipating your signal!"[30] The call for an aggressive war soon became louder: "The right which is not granted should be taken. By war?—Yes, when necessary, by war!"[31]

Pan-Turk activity during World War II extended beyond journalism. Nazi Germany had displayed some interest in the Turkic groups of the Soviet Union even before the outbreak of the war.[32] During the war, the Germans attempted to exploit Pan-Turk feelings to their own advantage—both in Europe and in Turkey. Appropriate Pan-Turk propaganda was directed toward Turkic groups in the Soviet Union,[33] and Turkic prisoners of war in German camps—numbering about 55,000— were drafted into fighting units with promises of liberation phrased in irredentist terms.[34] These units, constantly reinforced, eventually numbered hundreds of thousands.[35] In Turkey itself, the government remained cool toward German inducements. Therefore, Turkic immigrants in Ankara and Istanbul were used as intermediaries between

German Ambassador Franz von Papen and leading Pan-Turk activists. The latter stepped up their anticommunist and anti-Soviet propaganda as well as their demand for Turkey to join the Axis powers. A clash was inevitable, and on May 3, 1944, in open defiance of martial law, the Pan-Turk activists organized major anticommunist demonstrations in Ankara and Istanbul, with Atsiz, Sancar, and other leaders in the forefront. Pan-Turk slogans were abundantly in evidence.[36] The government reacted swiftly and vigorously by arresting the ringleaders and bringing them to trial, while banning the Pan-Turk organizations.

Public Pan-Turk activity thus failed again, but the trials afforded an excellent opportunity for irredentist propaganda within Turkey, as they enjoyed extensive and fully detailed press coverage. The Pan-Turkists, convicted and subsequently acquitted on appeal, commenced intensive political activity in the postwar era. In 1945 Turkey passed from a single-party to a multiparty regime,[37] which obviously offered new vistas for political organization. Later, the military intervention of 1960–1961 was followed by an era of relative liberalization: censorship of the press was relaxed and political groupings were permitted to organize and act rather freely. Political associations proliferated, including Pan-Turk groups. Several Pan-Turk periodicals of the interwar era were revived and others launched, books and pamphlets were published, seminars were convened, and public lectures were given. Initially there was no countrywide Pan-Turk organization, but in the 1950s and early 1960s local groups intensified their activity and kept in touch with other Pan-Turk groups.

Although the ideological makeup of these diverse groups varied, there were some common denominators in their propaganda. First, the formerly official doctrines of Kemalism could now be publicly challenged. Second, although race theories were propounded no more (or only rarely), as they had been discredited with the defeat of Nazi Germany, irredentism became a virtually constant source of inspiration for the Pan-Turks in Turkey. Such views appeared more acceptable in the postwar generation than during the first generation of the republic; after all, Turkey had since veered from neutrality toward an alliance with the West, cemented by U.S. economic aid, membership in NATO, and participation in the Korean War. Moreover, "Outside Turks" were having problems in Greece, Cyprus, Iraq, the Soviet Union, and elsewhere, and appeals for their liberation now found more favor with the masses in Turkey than before. Irredentism thus became the oft-repeated message of Pan-Turkists, whose clarion call for the reestablishment of the large Turkish-Turkic empire extending from the Mediterranean to the Pacific was sounded with increasing frequency. The more extreme among them, led by Atsiz and his disciples, undisguisedly called for war against Greece and the formation of a grand alliance for a future war against the Soviet Union.

As so much of Turkey's politics evolved around its political parties in the years following World War II, it was only a matter of time until a party with Pan-Turk principles would be launched. Its leader, Alparslan Türkeş, an "Outside Turk" born in Cyprus in 1917, moved to Istanbul at the age of fifteen, opted for a military career, and rose to the rank of colonel. In 1944, while on active service, he took part in Pan-Turk demonstrations and was tried along with other leaders, convicted, and then acquitted. In 1960, he was active in the military group that seized control of the government, but was later expelled from it. He resigned from the military and entered politics in 1963.[38] Two years later, realizing that the Pan-Turks were too few and too scattered to set up a political party on their own, Türkeş took over the leadership of an extant political party, the Republican Peasant and Nation party, whose name he later changed to the more appealing Nationalist Action party.[39] Although the party's fortunes are not relevant to this study, we note its performance in several electoral contests: eleven seats in the 1965 National Assembly (the Lower House), one seat in 1969, three in 1973, and sixteen in 1977.[40] Although the National Assembly had 450 members, the Nationalist Action party succeeded in entering cabinet coalitions in the years 1975–1977 and again in 1977–1980—with Türkeş as vice-premier. The military intervention of September 12, 1980 dissolved the parliament, and later (1981) all political parties as well.[41] Türkeş and other leaders of the Nationalist Action party were indicted for subversive activities, and their lengthy trial ended with several convictions.

Our primary concern is with the Pan-Turk irredentist views of Türkeş, which represented a component in the party's ideology. Once the party entered parliament and the cabinet, Pan-Turkism came out of the political wilderness into which it had been thrust by Mustafa Kemal and his associates and rejoined the mainstream of Turkish politics. However, one should remember, again, that Pan-Turkism was only one component in the Nationalist Action party's platform. When the party was in opposition, irredentist sentiment often found expression in Türkeş's speeches and written statements. The Turks of Cyprus, not surprisingly, constituted the focus of his passionate pleas for the "Outside Turks," whose universal liberation he advocated. His pronouncements remind one of earlier Pan-Turk propaganda, characteristic of anti-Greek and anticommunist (as well as anti-Soviet) positions. Understandably, perhaps, Türkeş toned down his style considerably when serving in the cabinet, refraining from irredentist declarations that would have embarrassed the government. This caused a rift between him and many of his Pan-Turk supporters, who left the party demonstratively. The Pan-Turks have now reverted to their peripheral position in the Republic of Turkey and have exerted little impact during military rule in 1980–1983 and the subsequent return to civilian government. Apparently, their number has decreased radically and their efforts now concentrate primarily on journalistic propaganda.

CONCLUDING REMARKS

The following observations establish a tentative typology of irredentism as expressed in Pan-Turkism and compare several of its features with those expressed in irredentist movements and ideologies elsewhere.[42]

1. Pan-Turk ideology originated in the diaspora and was propounded in the home country (the Ottoman Empire, then the Republic of Turkey) only later. In this respect, it appears to resemble Pan-Arabism, which was first preached by Syrian émigrés in Western Europe, or Pan-Slavism, whose inception occurred outside Czarist Russia (the first Pan-Slavic Congress convened in Prague in 1848), but differs from Pan-Italianism, Pan-Hellenism, and Pan-Germanism, all of which began in their respective home countries.[43]

2. The inception of Pan-Turkism unfolded on the cultural plane with emphasis on such disciplines as language, history, literature, folklore, and archaeology, common to all Turkish-Turkic groups. The irredentist element surfaced only later when political considerations set in, whereupon research and literary works on those disciplines began discussing "liberation" of the "Outside Turks" and annexation of their territories. The trend is frequently from the moderate to the extreme. This process appears familiar to many other Pan-ideologies. Pan-Arabism, for example, began as a literary and linguistic movement active in cultural clubs in Syria and elsewhere in the late nineteenth century, but reached its clearest irredentist expression in the Pan-Arabism that is now a principal component of the doctrines of the Baath party governing Iraq and Syria. The Iraqi attack on Iran in 1980 was partly explained as stemming from a desire to free and annex the Arab population in Iran's border district (which the Iraqis call Arabistan and the Iranians call Khozistan). The Syrian leadership, in turn, seeks to create a Greater Syria comprising Lebanon, Israel, Jordan, and southern Turkey (which the Syrians call Alexandretta and the Turks call Hatay). This observation also applies to Pan-Hellenism, which started as a cultural renaissance and developed politically into an irredentist Megali Idea aiming at the annexation of Asia Minor (now in Turkey), which is the home of several Greek communities and was once part of the Greek Empire. Pan-Germanism, likewise cultural at first, aimed at colonial expansion at the end of the nineteenth century and degenerated

into Hitler's renewed version, which aimed at and succeeded in annexing the Sudetenland, Austria, and several other lands claimed to be part of the German *Heimat*.

3. Pan-Turk irredentism is evidently romantic and emotional; basically, however, it is not irrational, but rather possesses a rationale of its own. Because Pan-Turkism is largely motivated by cultural, ethnic, and political considerations, it has tended to ignore: (1) geographical factors (contiguousness or the lack thereof has never been an argument); (2) military situations (the might of the Soviet Union has not deterred Pan-Turkism in Turkey); (3) economic considerations (raised only in rare instances and somewhat apologetically, as it was thought that they should not constitute a motivation for nationalism); and (4) religious matters (in Russia and elsewhere the Turkic groups were divided between Sunnis and Shiites, whereas the Republic of Turkey prided itself on its secularism and passed laws banning the mixing of religion and politics; moreover, Islam was not particular to the Turks alone). It would appear that many of these attitudes of romantic emotionalism and apparent irrationalism were manifest in other irredentist Pan-ideologies, with the exception of Pan-Germanism (which was definitely economic-minded in its early years) and several other ideologies that turned to religion for a while: early Pan-Slavism, although not since its revival by Stalin after the German attack in 1941; Pan-Hellenism at first, but not at present; and Pan-Arabism, which used to express itself in Islamic terms but has ceased doing so in its current (Baath) version. It thus appears that over time there has been a gradual weakening of the religious element in irredentism, which now approaches the Turkish model in this aspect as well.

4. Pan-Turk irredentism has consistently maintained and fostered a "villain image" of its principal opponent, that is, the factor chiefly responsible for subjugating "Outside Turks" and their territories, which may comprise one or more states or peoples. Initially it was Czarist Russia and, to a lesser degree, China; then the Soviet Union and, to a lesser degree, Iraq and Iran; later, with the rising tensions over Cyprus, it became Greece (a book attacking the Megali Idea was published in Ankara as recently as 1985)[44] and currently Bulgaria (where the local Turkish population is allegedly compelled to change its personal names and lose its identity).[45] The villain image has obviously been germane to every irredentist ideology known to us: Pan-Arabism had the Ottoman Turks, then Israel; Pan-Slavism the Germans; Pan-Germanism, the Slavs; Pan-Italianism, the Austro-Hungarians and later the Yugoslavs (over Trieste); Pan-Hellenism, the Turks; Hungarian irredentism, the Romanians (over Transylvania); Romanian irredentism, the Hungarians (over Transylvania) and later the Soviets (over Bessarabia, now called the Moldavian Soviet Republic); and Albanian irredentism had

Yugoslavia (over the Kosovo district). Even so, it would seem that Turkish irredentism has had more than its share of villains to contest with (perhaps because of the nature of the Turkish-Turkic diaspora).

5. Organization appears to have been a main weakness of irredentist Pan-Turkism. Although no precise data are available regarding the size and composition of its membership, one may gauge its range from several hundred, at present, to several thousand during World War I and again in the 1970s. Pan-Turk speeches and writings indicate that the movement, which comprised competing small groups, was tightknit and elitist, led by intellectuals and supported by students and middle-class townspeople. It emphasized written and oral propaganda, with newspapers serving as rallying points for each group, supplemented by cultural meetings featuring lectures, music, and performances. Available information indicates that this situation is no different from that of other irredentist Pan-movements, with the possible exception of the Pan-German League, which reached its peak in 1901 with 21,924 members.[46] Otherwise, irredentist Pan-movements seem to have generally resembled Pan-Turkism in scope and organization.[47]

6. Finally, irredentism in Turkey has evidently failed to achieve its objectives so far, probably due to a variety of reasons, both internal and external. Among the former are poor organization; limited public support; an ideology phrased in too elaborate terms; and the inability to mobilize government support and commitment (in the only instance in which Pan-Turkism did find favor with the state leadership, during World War I, this leadership allied itself with the losing side). Among the latter are the relatively greater power of some of Turkey's neighbors, chiefly the Soviet Union (when Turkey was stronger, as in 1974, it did not hesitate to risk war with Greece over Cyprus, where it established a new Turkish political entity); the particular makeup of Turkic groups abroad (where they are dispersed among other ethnic minorities, often at great distance from one another); and the energetic pursuit by the Turkish republic of a policy of peace and improvement of relations with its immediate neighbors.[48] It is tempting to compare this case with the failure of other irredentist movements and ideologies, such as Pan-Arabism, Pan-Germanism, Pan-Hellenism, or Hungarian and Albanian irredentism, or with the relative success of others, such as Pan-Italianism or Romanian irredentism. This subject, however, obviously requires additional research.

NOTES

1. In the Tarihi Araştirmalar ve Dokümantasyon Merkezleri Kurma ve Gelistirme Vakfi.
2. Myron Weiner, "The Macedonian Syndrome: An Historical Model of

International Relations and Political Development," *World Politics* 13, 4 (July 1971): 665–683.

3. S. A. Zenkovsky, "A Century of Tatar Revival," *American Slavic and East European Review* 12 (October 1953): 303–318.

4. Alexandre Bennigsen and Chantal Quelquejay, *Les mouvements nationaux chez les Musulmans de Russie* (Paris and The Hague: Mouton, 1960), pp. 28ff., 40.

5. Vincent Monteil, *Les Musulmans soviétiques* (Paris: Seuil, 1957), p. 22; A. Vambery, "The Awakening of the Tatars," *The Nineteenth Century* (London) 57 (February 1905): 217–227.

6. H. C. d'Encausse, *Réforme et révolution chez les Musulmans de l'Empire russe* (Paris: Fondation Nationale des Sciences Politiques, 1966), pp. 103–104.

7. The only detailed study of this language to date seems to be Gustav Burbice's "Die Sprache Ismail Bey Gaspyralys," unpublished doctoral thesis, Hamburg University, 1950.

8. G. V. Mende, *Der nationale Kampf der Russlandtürken* (Berlin: Seminar Für Orientalische Sprachen, 1936), p. 93.

9. For Gasprinsky's lifework and impact, see, in addition to materials in the previous notes, Cafer Seydahmet Kirimer, *Gaspirali Ismail Bey* (Istanbul, 1934); Ahmet Caferoğlu, *Ismail Gaspirali. Öümünün 50. Yildönümü münasebetile bir etüd* (Istanbul, 1964).

10. For these three congresses, see A. V. Pyaskovskiy, *Ryevolutsiya 1905–1907 godov v Tyurkyestanye* (Moscow, 1958), pp. 98–102, 543ff.; R. A. Pierce, *Russian Central Asia, 1867–1917: A Study in Colonial Rule* (Berkeley and Los Angeles: University of California Press, 1960), pp. 255–258.

11. Mende, *Der nationale Kampf*, pp. 71ff.

12. David Thomas, "Yusuf Akçura and the Intellectual Origins of Üç tarz-i siyaset," *Journal of Turkish Studies* 2 (1978): 127–140; François Georgeon, *Aux origines du nationalisme turc: Yusuf Akçura* (Paris: Institute d'Etude Anatoliennes, Editions ADPF, 1980).

13. George Macartney, "Bolshevism as I Saw It in Tashkent in 1918," *Journal of the Central Asian Society* 7 (1920), esp. p. 42; Mustafa Chokaev, "The Basmaji Movement in Turkestan," *Asiatic Review* (London) 24 (April 1928): 273–288; P. Galuzo and F. Bodzhko, *Vosstaniye 1916 v Sryednyey Azii* (Moscow, 1932); A. Oktay, *Türkestan milî hareketi ve Mustafa Çokay* (Istanbul, 1950); Edige Kirimal, *Der nationale Kampf der Krimtürken mit besondere Besichtigung der Jahr 1917-1918* (Emsdetten: Lechte, 1952), pp. 37–277; Geoffrey Wheeler, *The Modern History of Soviet Central Asia* (Westport, Conn.: Greenwood Press, 1975); Z. D. Kastyel'skaya, *Iz istorii Tyurkestanskogo kraya (1865–1917)* (Moscow, 1980), pp. 89–99.

14. G. J. Massell, *The Surrogate Proletariat: Moslem Women and Revolutionary Strategists in Soviet Central Asia, 1919–1929* (Princeton: Princeton University Press, 1974), pp. 32–34.

15. Jacob M. Landau, *Pan-Turkism in Turkey* (London: C. Hurst, 1981), pp. 28ff.

16. A recent bibliography lists 436 item. I. Binark and N. Sefercioğlu, *Doğumunun 95. münasebetiyle Ziya Gökalp bibliyografiyasi: kitap, makale* (Ankara, 1971).

17. The most detailed works about Gökalp remain Uriel Heyd, *Foundations of Turkish Nationalism: The Life and Teachings of Ziya Gökalp* (London: Luzac, 1950) and Niyazi Berkes, *Turkish Nationalism and Western Civilization:*

Selected Essays of Ziya Gökalp (New York: Columbia University Press, 1959). Gökalp's main book was translated into English by Robert Devereux as *The Principles of Turkism* (Leiden: Brill, 1968).

18. Tekin Alp, *Türkismus und Pantürkismus* (Weimar: Deutsche Orientbücherei, 1915).

19. For further details, see Jacob M. Landau, *Tekinalp: Turkish Patriot 1883-1961* (Istanbul and Leiden: Nederlands Archeological-Historical Institute, 1984), esp. pp. 25–27, 99–102, 273–278.

20. Jacob M. Landau, "Pan-Islam and Pan-Turkism During the Final Years of the Ottoman Empire: Some Considerations," in Robert Hillenbrand, ed., *Proceedings, Union Européenne des Arabisants et Islamisants, 10th Congress, Edinburgh, September 9–16, 1980* (Edinburgh, 1982), pp. 43–45.

21. For instance, in Medina, in 1917. See Public Record Office (London), FO (Foreign Office series) 395/139, file 15725, no. 144185, decoded message from Sir Reginald Wingate to the Foreign Office, dated Ramleh, July 21, 1917.

22. C. J. Walker, *Armenia: The Survival of a Nation* (London: Croom Helm, 1980), p. 191.

23. See the archival sources mentioned in Landau, *Pan-Turkism in Turkey*, pp. 49ff. and 65–66.

24. Quoted by Harry Luke, *The Making of Modern Turkey* (London, 1936), p. 161.

25. Louis Fischer, "The End of Enver Pasha," *Virginia Quarterly Review* (University of Virginia) 6, 2 (April 1930): 232–239; and P. R. Ali, "Enver Pasha: His Status in Modern Turkish History," *Egyptian Historical Review* (Cairo) 22 (1975), esp. pp. 24–27.

26. Details are found in Jacob M. Landau, ed., *Ataturk and the Modernization of Turkey* (Boulder, Colo.: Westview Press, 1984).

27. On Atsiz see, besides his numerous writings, a biography by Altan Deliorman, *Tanidiğim Atsiz* (Istanbul, 1978), and a memorial volume in his honor, Erel Güngör et al., eds., *Atsiz armağani* (Istanbul, 1976).

28. Hüseyin Nihal Atsiz, "Yirminci asirda Türk meselesi," *Orhun*, 9 (July 16, 1934), esp. pp. 157–160.

29. See examples in the following Pan-Turk periodicals: *Bozkurt* (December 1940): 208–213, (March 1942): 6; *Tanridağ* 3 (May 22, 1942): 4–7, (August 21, 1942): 11–13, (August 28, 1942): 6–7.

30. *Bozkurt* 11 (July 1941): 249.

31. Bozkurt 2nd series, no. 1 (March 5, 1942): 6.

32. See "Les puissances et la politique turco-tatare," *Politique Etrangère* (Paris) 3, 3 (June 1938): 236–241.

33. Archives of the German Foreign Office, Büro des Staatssekretärs, Panturan adh. 1941, file Büro Pers. M. See also *Akten zur Deutschen Auswärtigen Politik 1918–1945, Serie D. 1937–1941* 13, 2 (1970): 467–470, dated September 26, 1941, Berlin.

34. Archives of the German Foreign Office, ibid., dated December 22, 1941.

35. Details in C. W. Hostler, *Turkism and the Soviets: The Turks of the World and Their Political Objectives* (London: George Allen & Unwin, 1957), pp. 177ff.; Lothar Krecker, *Deutschland und die Türkei im Zweiten Weltkrieg* (Frankfurt am Main: Frankfurter Wissenschaftliche Beiträge, 1964), p. 220, estimates them at 200,000.

36. For the whole affair, see Public Record Office, FO 371/44133, R 7715/

789/44, Ambassador Knatchbull-Hugessen's no. 173, "confidential," to Eden, dated May 6, 1944, Ankara.

37. The most detailed work on this change is K. H. Karpat's *Turkey's Politics: The Transition to a Multi-Party System* (Princeton: Princeton University Press, 1959).

38. In addition to Türkeş's own writings and speeches, several biographies of him are available, such as M. Özdag, *Alparslan Türkeş* (Ankara, 1965); Fuat Uluç, *İşte liderler* (Ankara, 1965), esp. pp. 13ff.; Bekir Berk and N. M. Polat, *Islamî hareket ve Türkeş* (N.p. [Istanbul], 1969).

39. The only two studies of this party available to date are Jacob M. Landau, "The Militant Right in Turkish Politics," in J. M. Landau, *Middle Eastern Themes: Papers in History and Politics* (London: Frank Cass, 1973), pp. 277–289; and Jacob M. Landau, "The Nationalist Action Party in Turkey," *Journal of Contemporary History* (London) 17, 4 (October 1982): 587–606.

40. For details, see Jacob M. Landau, E. Özbudun, and F. Tachau, eds., *Electoral Politics in the Middle East: Issues, Voters and Elites* (London: Croom Helm/Stanford, Calif.: Hoover Institution, 1980).

41. For which see M. Ali Birand, *12 Eylül saat: 04.00* (n.p., 1984).

42. There are as yet only few (and hardly satisfactory) comparative studies of Pan-movements and fewer of irredentism. See, for example, Karl Haushoffer, *Geopolitik der Pan-Ideen* (Berlin: Zentral-Verlag, 1931); Hans Kohn, "Pan-Movements," *Encyclopaedia of Social Sciences* 11 (1931), s.v.; and F. Kazemzadeh, "Pan Movements," *International Encyclopaedia of Social Sciences* 11 (1968), s.v.

43. See, for example, Michel Laissy, *Du Panarabisme à la Ligue arabe* (Paris: G. P. Maisonneuve, 1948); Shaukat Ali, *Pan-Movements in the Third World: Pan-Arabism, Pan-Africanism, Pan-Islamism* (Lahore: Publishers United, n.d. [1976]); Fouad Ajami, "The End of Pan-Arabism," *Foreign Affairs* 57, 2 (Winter 1978); M. B. Petrovich, *The Emergence of Russian Pan-Slavism, 1856–1870* (New York: Columbia University Press, 1956); Hans Kohn, *Pan-Slavism in Its History and Ideology*, 2nd ed. (New York: University of Notre Dame Press, 1960); Th. G. Tatsios, *The Megali Idea and the Greek-Turkish War of 1897: The Impact of the Cretan Problem on Greek Irredentism, 1866–1897*, unpublished doctoral thesis, Columbia University, New York, 1973; R. G. Usher, *Pan-Germanism* (London: Constable, 1914); M. S. Wertheimer, *The Pan-German League, 1890–1914* (New York: Studies in History, 1971).

44. *Türk-Yunan ilişkileri ve Megalo Idea* (Ankara: Ankara University Press, 1985). This book—intentionally, no doubt—retails for a mere T.L. 90 (= US $0.16).

45. Numerous publications have recently appeared on this. See, for example, the collection of lectures entitled *Ankara Üniversitesi Bulgaristan'da Türkler semineri (10 nisan 1985)* (Ankara, 1985).

46. Wertheimer, *The Pan-German League*, pp. 95ff.

47. Other Pan-movements may have had even fewer members than Pan-Turkism. See data in W. J. Argyle, "Size and Scale as Factors in the Development of Nationalist Movements," in A. D. Smith, ed., *Nationalist Movements* (New York: St. Martin's Press, 1976), pp. 31–53.

48 See also Jacob M. Landau, "The Fortunes and Misfortunes of Pan-Turkism," *Central Asian Society* (Oxford) 7, 1 (1988): 1–5.

CHAPTER 7

Irredentism and Politics in Africa

BENYAMIN NEUBERGER

Every divided country or partitioned people is unhappy.

—Leo Tolstoy

In Chapter 1, Donald Horowitz defines irredentism as a "movement by members of an ethnic group in one state to retrieve ethnically kindred people and their territory across borders." He discusses two basic forms of irredentism, describing the first as "an attempt to detach land and people from one state in order to incorporate them in another" and the other as "an attempt to detach land and people divided among more than one state in order to incorporate them in a single new state." In both cases, "irredentism involves subtracting from one state and adding to another state, new or already existing," whereas "secession involves subtracting alone."

Horowitz's definition, however, has some basic flaws. The major mistake is to define the creation of any "new state" as a form of irredentism. A new state is also involved in every case of secession, so that if we want to preserve the distinction between secession and irredentism we must make clear that irredentism means an attempt made by an existing state to "redeem" territories and peoples it considers its own. Horowitz himself later admits that his definition is problematical when he says that "to define irredentism as an attempt to retrieve kindred people across boundaries is to assume that kindred people know each other, that kinship and ethnicity are firm. It is by now well established, however, that ethnic identity is variable over time and context."

To analyze irredentism in Africa we do need a more sophisticated classification of irredenta. The original Italian term *terra irredenta* means "territory to be redeemed." It presupposes a redeeming state as well as such a territory. The redeeming state can be an ethnocultural nation-state, a historic state, or a multiethnic plural state. The territory to be redeemed is sometimes regarded as part of an ethnocultural homeland, as part of a historic state, or as an integral part of one geographical whole. Even theoretically, the various kinds of redeeming states and territories to be redeemed create different kinds of irredenta; but reality is still more complex because many irredenta are "mixed" and disputes about the nature of the ethnocultural nation, the historic state, and the geographical whole often arise. Classifying the different kinds of redeeming states and *terra irredenta* would nevertheless enable us to cover all the major cases of irredentism in postcolonial Africa.

The potential for irredentism in Africa is considerable, and we agree with Asiwaju that the partition of Africa is "far from being a closed matter."[1] Political surgery partitioned hundreds of ethnic groups during the colonial scramble for Africa. Most groups were divided into two parts, but some were split up among three, four, or even five states (for example, the Somalis, Bakongo, Ewe, Zande, Fulani, Ngoni, Chewa, Lunda, and Yao). Many of these partitioned groups have preserved a "dormant or active sense of community" based on common language, religion, culture, kinship ties, and political leadership. The fact that in many of Africa's plural states one ethnic group or an ethnic coalition rules and other ethnic groups feel left out and oppressed, and the fact that large modernization gaps exist between the various groups, create conditions that could be conducive to separatism and irredentism. Irredentists argue that Africa's boundaries are artificial and colonial, and that its peoples are subject to internal colonialism. They therefore effectively mobilize the language of anticolonialism and base their claims on the universally accepted principle of national self-determination.

The best-known case of irredentist aspiration in Africa is the Somali endeavor to achieve a Greater Somalia by adding the Somali-inhabited territories of Ethiopia (Ogaden) and Kenya (the former Northern Frontier District) as well as the state of Djibouti to the Somali nation-state. The Somali case contains all the ingredients of "classical" irredentism, including ethnic fragments across the borders and organized nationalist movements struggling to achieve unification with the "mother country."

Underlying the demand for a Greater Somalia is the strong feeling that all Somalis are one nation. Former Somali President Haj Mohammed Hussein emphasized that "we are the same geographically and racially. We have the same language and the same religion. There is no future for us except as part of a Greater Somalia."[2] Somalis define their nation in terms reminiscent of nineteenth-century European nationalism. Hussein Adam defines the Somalis as a people inhabiting a contiguous territory and possessing a common language, culture, history, and tradition, with Islam providing "an important ingredient of their common culture."[3] Somalis perceive the Somali nation in Somalia, Ethiopia, Kenya, and Djibouti as one "organic" whole. A popular Somali liberation song asks, "How can an amputated man sleep comfortably at night?"[4] Somali nationalists are determined never to "sleep" until the "amputated" parts are "returned" to Somalia. As in Italian, German, and Polish nineteenth-century nationalism, for Somalis too the rallying cry is "all the nation in one state." In 1981, the Somali information minister declared that all Somalis "are one and have the right to be unified."[5] In the name of Somali unity the Legislative Council of British Somaliland, claiming to represent the "proper feeling in the country,"[6] decided in 1960 to merge with Italian Somalia. Somalia's constitution maintains the demands (also reflected in the flag of the Somali Republic with its five stars) for a union of all Somali territories. Somalia has since then fought two bitter irredentist wars with Ethiopia (in 1964 and 1977) and has been involved in guerrilla warfare in both Kenya and Ethiopia.

The three "BLS" nation-states (Botswana, Lesotho, and Swaziland) also have a strong irredentist potential. In all three states, the "nation" is divided between the nation-state and South Africa. The Swazis, Sotho, and Tswana live in South Africa either in distinct homelands or in so-called "white South Africa."

The first serious irredentist effort was made by Swaziland in the early 1980s when it tried to make a "land deal" with South Africa and to incorporate the Swazi homeland of KaNgwane and the Ingwavuma District of Kwazulu.[7] In the Swazi case, the national Swazi kingdom never recognized the colonial boundary established in the 1880s between the Transvaal and Swaziland. Many of South Africa's Swazis continued for decades to regard themselves as loyal subjects of the Swazi king. Since the 1930s a Swazi cultural nationalism has grown on both sides of the border, leading to the publication of the first Swazi newspaper (1934), the first book on Swazi history (1939), the first grammar of the Swazi language (1952), and the introduction of Swazi as a medium of instruction in the schools of Swaziland (1969) and KaNgwane (1978). The "land deal" of 1982 was supported by the Swazi government and the Inyatsiya ya Mswati party in KaNgwane, but it was aborted by the opposition of the KaNgwane and Kwazulu governments.

Another nation-state that has followed an ethnic irredentist policy is the Libyan Arab Republic. Qaddafi rejected the colonial boundaries that divide "brothers" and called for the unification of all Sahara Arabs (including other Muslim and partially Arabized peoples like the Berbers and Touaregs) within a Greater Libya, as a first step to a larger Arab unity. This at least partially explains Libyan territorial ambitions toward portions of Tunisia, Nigeria, Mali, Niger, and Chad.

Libyan ambitions in Chad clearly illustrate Libyan irredentism. In the 1970s and 1980s, Libya attempted to annex the Aouzou Strip and sometimes the whole Borku-Ennedi-Tibesti (B.E.T.) region. In 1981 it even tried to annex the whole of Chad. Libyan aspirations have direct relevance to the ethnic Arab presence in Chad and to the perception of other Muslim Chadian peoples (like the Toubou, Massalit, and Kanembou) as Arab and even Libyan. Many of the pro-Libyan forces in Chad were Arab and were led by Arabs like Asil Ahmat, Cheikh Ibn Omar, Mahamat Dana, Abba Siddic, and Abdalhi Adoum.[8]

Irredentist aspirations have also been strong among the Ewe people in the Togo Republic and the Volta Region of Ghana. The Ewe share a common myth of descent and a common language, culture, and history, and belong to the Ewe Presbyterian Church. Their ethnic homeland stretches from the Mano River in Benin to the Volta River in Ghana. In the 1890s they were divided into three; the majority went to German Togoland, and the minorities became part of French Dahomey (Benin) and the British Gold Coast (Ghana). After World War I, German Togoland was again partitioned into French Togo (today's Togo Republic) and British Togoland (today part of Ghana's Volta Region).

Since the 1930s, political parties and other organizations in both British Togoland and French Togo have been calling either for Ewe unification or for the unification of the two Togos. Since its independence in 1960, the Togo Republic has intermittently followed an irredentist policy toward former British Togoland. Togo is not an Ewe nation-state, but in the early 1960s, the Ewe were politically dominant and, under the leadership of the Ewe nationalist, Sylvanus Olympio, Togo acted as a quasi Ewe nation-state. The current non-Ewe administration of Gnassingbe Eyadema continued its support for the irredentist Togoland Liberation Movement (TOLIMO) operation in Ghana in the 1970s and 1980s, but its emphasis shifted from pan-Ewe nationalism to Togoland territorialism—the supra-ethnic demand to reestablish a united Togo in its pre–World War I colonial boundaries.

In 1956, a plebiscite was conducted by the United Nations in the Ghanaian part of Togo in order to ascertain the wishes of the population. In the territory as a whole the majority opted for unity with Ghana, but the southern Ewe districts overwhelmingly voted against this. The irredentist demands of (French) Togo have enjoyed strong popular support in the Ewe parts of British Togo. In the 1960s, the response to Togolese irredentism was "irredentism in reverse" by Nkrumah's Ghana,[9] a demand by the Ghanaian plural state that the Togolese Ewe (and the Ivory Coast Agni) be incorporated within a Ghana that would absorb peoples who were outside Ghana but linked by "natural ethnic affinity" with the Ghanaian people.[10]

Another case of ethnic irredentism in postcolonial Africa was the Mauritanian effort in the mid-1970s to establish a Greater Mauritania based on the Hassaniya Arabs of Mauritania and the Western Sahara.

The founding president of Mauritania, Mokhtar Ould Daddah, called for the "reunification" of all Hassaniya-speakers who have shared a common "desert civilization" and have been divided by "artificial colonial boundaries."[11]

The redeeming state is a nation-state in the Somali and Swazi cases and a quasi nation-state dominated by one ethnic group in Togo and Mauritania. Another variant of irredentism is the Afar case, where the redeeming state is the binational Somali-Afar state of Djibouti. Here the goals of Afari nationalism are to transform Djibouti into an Afari nation-state, and then create a Greater Danakilia by attaching to it the Afari-inhabited areas of Ethiopia (parts of Eritrea, Tigre, Wollo, and Hararge).[12]

/ Similar irredentist aspirations were voiced by the Gabonese Fang, who wished to unite with fellow Fang in Rio Muni (now part of Equatorial Guinea), and by the "big three" in Nigeria—the Ibos, Yorubas, and Hausas—who have intermittently voiced demands for unification with "brothers and sisters" across the border (the Ibos in Cameroon and Fernando Poo, the Hausa in Niger, and the Yoruba in Benin).[13]

European irredenta—whether German, Italian, Greek, Spanish, Russian, or Polish—have always been a combination of ethnic longing for national unification and attempts to restore historic states and historic boundaries, sometimes far beyond the ethnic boundaries. The same is true for African irredentism. Ethiopia—whether Haile Selassie's "empire" or Mengistu Haile Mariam's revolutionary republic—strongly believes in the need to preserve the unity of a historical Ethiopia.

Ethiopians have seen Ethiopia's unification with Eritrea in 1952 as a "return to the mother country," not as annexation.[14] "The history of Eritrea has been one with Ethiopia," declared the Ethiopian government in 1945.[15] The Ethiopian nationalists argued that the historical roots of Ethiopia were in Eritrean Axum and that it had been the center of the kingdom for a millennium.

Historical rationale was also used by Haile Selassie in the 1960s to explain his annexationist ambitions toward Djibouti, "one of Ethiopia's last provinces along the Red Sea."[16] In 1941, after Ethiopia's liberation from Italian rule, Haile Selassie even talked about the restoration of Benadir (Somalia) to historical Ethiopia.[17] In 1949, Ethiopia demanded the incorporation of the whole of Somalia into the Ethiopian Empire. In the early 1960s, the claim was dropped, but the Ethiopian emperor observed that "things would have been quite different according to history," thus indirectly maintaining the historic claim.[18] In 1964, the Third Division of the Ethiopian army was already on its way to Somali Hargeisa when the government decided not to invade Somalia. In 1978, the possibility of an Ethiopian invasion of Somalia was again openly discussed, and one should not rule out that an Ethiopian conquest could have revived the historical irredentist claims to Somali territory.

The Moroccan irredenta and its dream of a Greater Morocco within Morocco's historical boundaries are another illustration of the persistent influence of precolonial history, goals, and sentiments. The Moroccan irredenta led to wars with Algeria and to the protracted and bloody conflict in the Western Sahara. Essentially, the Moroccans wanted to restore the boundaries of the ancient Almoravid Empire of the eleventh and twelfth centuries. That goal led them at various times to claim the whole of Mauritania, the Western Sahara, portions of Algeria and Mali, and the Spanish enclaves of Ceuta and Melilla. In addition, they have already absorbed Spanish Northern and Southern Morocco, Tangier, and Ifni. In the 1960s, Morocco labeled independent Mauritania Morocco's "amputated part."[19] Istiqlal leader Allal al-Fassi drew a parallel between the idea of national self-determination for Mauritania and the notion that Liverpool or Marseilles should be granted the right to independent statehood.[20]

The present war in the Western Sahara stems from the deep-seated Moroccan conviction that the "Moroccan" Sahara is part of a historical Morocco liberated by Moroccan troops in 1976. The Moroccans argue that in precolonial times the tribes of the Western Sahara traditionally declared their allegiance to the Sultan of Morocco, whom they regarded as ruler and *amir-al' mu' minin* ("defender of the faithful"). The Sultan also appointed *qaids* (governors) of the Western Sahara tribes by *zahirs* (official pronouncements). Historical memories of past "glories and conquests" motivated the Moroccans to reconquer the Western Sahara and "return" it to Moroccan sovereignty.[21]

Another North African example of historical irredentism in the 1940s and early 1950s is the Egyptian claim to the Sudan, based on the perceived historical unity of the Nile Valley. A Southern African example of such historical irredentist claims is the Malawian dream to restore the historic Maravi Empire (including parts of Zambia and Mozambique) of the Chewa people, who are also dominant in modern Malawi.[22]

An overwhelming majority of the African political establishment, including most African governments and the OAU, reaffirms its commitment to the successor state of the colonial state by proclaiming the "sanctity" of the colonial borders and of the postcolonial state-system. Nevertheless, irredentism is sometimes based on the will of the postcolonial state to "redeem" territories that in the past were part of a larger colonial state. The movement for the reunification of both Togos and the re-creation of a German Togoland was one example, but in the Togolese case the hidden motivation behind Togolese irredentism was ethnic pan-Ewe nationalism. A "purer" case of such nonethnic irredentism is Cameroonian nationalism.

Before the German conquest of the 1880s, Cameroon had been a "conglomeration of ethnic communities."[23] It was neither a nation-state nor a historic state. The German colonial period produced a certain "sense of oneness." Decades after German Kamerun had been partitioned into French Cameroun and the British Cameroons, a strong irredentist movement arose in both parts of Cameroon that aimed to reunite the French and British parts of the former German entity.

In French Cameroun the radical nationalist Union des Populations du Cameroun (UPC) fought for independence and reunification from the time of its foundation in 1948. Its leader, Felix Roland Moumié, propagated the myth that Cameroon had been one since the days of old Carthago. The UPC nationalists declared that "Camerounians have always, are always and will always regard the French and British Cameroons as a single territory."[24] In the late 1950s, all the major political groupings in French Cameroun adopted the twin nationalist goals of independence and reunification. Ahmadu Ahidjo, who was to become the first president of independent Cameroon, demanded the *"reconstitution du Cameroun arbitrairement divisé."*[25] In both parts of Cameroon, parties using the German name Kamerun were formed so as to demonstrate the commitment to reunification of the former German colony (examples are the Kamerun United National Congress, the Kamerun National Democratic party, the Kamerun People's party, and the Kamerun National Convention).

After the 1960 plebiscite in the British Cameroons, the French Cameroun and the Southern British Cameroons united, and the Northern British Cameroons voted to join Nigeria. In the 1960s and 1970s, the Cameroon republic nevertheless maintained its irredentist claims toward the former British Northern Cameroons. The Cameroonian parliament was united in its insistent demands that Nigeria "return" the Northern Cameroons. During Ahidjo's presidency, Cameroon annually observed a day of mourning to commemorate the loss of the Northern Cameroons. Ahidjo insisted that the Cameroonians were determined *"de retrouver leur frontieres du passé."* The case of Cameroonian irredentism is a vivid example of nonethnic irredentism in which a plural state attempts to redeem territories in order to re-create a former colonial state that was not a precolonial historic state like Ethiopia, Morocco, or Egypt.

Another such example of nonethnic irredentism is the case of the Comoro Islands. The redeeming state is the Comoro republic, which consists of the islands of Grande Comoro, Anjouan, and Moheli, and the territory to be redeemed is the island of Mayotte, which was detached from the Comoro colonial state in 1979 and became a French *Territoire d'outre mer* (TOM). Comorian nationalists regard Mayotte as an integral part of the Comoros and want to reunify it with the other three islands, even though the majority on Mayotte prefers separatism under French sovereignty.

Sometimes irredentism has its origin in geography—in the belief that the redeeming state and the territories to be redeemed form one geographic whole. There is, for instance, a strong tendency in the Third World to deny the right of national self-determination to colonial enclaves like Goa, Macao, and Hong Kong. Irredentist aspirations toward enclaves were already successful when Morocco united with Ifni and Tangier and when Benin annexed Sao João Baptista de Ajundá. Current claims include the enclaves of Ceuta and Melilla (Morocco), Cabinda (Congo and Zaire), and Walfish Bay (Namibia). Senegalese claims to Gambia are also influenced by the enclave nature of Gambia, which is surrounded by Senegal on all sides.

We may sum up the analysis of the African irredenta by emphasizing the need to differentiate between various types of redeeming states, such as nation-states (e.g., Somalia), quasi nation-states (e.g., Togo), historic states (e.g., Ethiopia), or plural states (e.g., Cameroon). We have also demonstrated that territories to be redeemed may be defined by ethnicity (e.g., Ogaden), precolonial history (e.g., Eritrea), colonial history (e.g., Northern Cameroons), or geography (e.g., Walfish Bay).

Further questions center on why so few cases of irredentism exist in Africa and why most of the irredenta have failed to achieve their goals up to now.

Most European irredenta involved true nation-states (e.g., Germany, Italy, or France) or quasi nation-states in which one nation was clearly predominant (e.g., Poland, Hungary, Spain). In these cases, the state attempted to redeem a *terra irredenta* with ethnic "brothers" across the boundary. In Black Africa there are very few nation-states and quasi nation-states, and the likelihood for a state's active involvement in irredentism is therefore greatly diminished. Most ethnic groups, divided between two states by an international boundary, are not candidates for irredentism for the very reason that they do not regard the two states as "theirs." In that sense we agree with Phiri that "partitioned ethnic groups are often bound by community feeling but they 'belong' to neither one state or the other . . . they 'belong' to themselves."[26] The Masai in Kenya and Tanzania, the Lunda in Zaire and Zambia, the Yoruba in Nigeria and Benin, and the Toucouleur in Senegal and Mauritania are indeed very different from the Sudeten Germans in the 1930s, the Catholic Irish in Ulster, or the Alsatians or the Austro-Germans in South Tyrol. African ethnic minorities who feel dominated and oppressed in one plural state have no incentive to become irredentist and join another plural state in which they may be equally dominated and oppressed. That is why the Toubous in Chad did not strive to join Libya in the 1960s and 1970s, why the Kenyan Oromos have no wish to join their brothers in Ethiopia (or vice versa), and why the Sudanese

Zande do not have the inclination to be annexed by Zaire or the Central African Republic.

Horowitz's rule that "if the retrieving group does not have a strong position in the putative irredentist state, its claims will be ignored or suppressed"[27] clearly applies to most "unhappy" partitioned groups in Black Africa because "only rarely did partitioned groups wield much influence within a state that the state identified with their ethos, thus becoming virtually a nation-state."[28] The exceptions to this African rule (Somalia, Swaziland, and Togo, for example) did indeed produce irredentist movements and aspirations. Another factor that should not be ignored is that most partitioned groups are small, weak, and peripheral, compared to the size of the population and the power of the state to which they belong; therefore, their chances to successfully break away from the state are slim.

Another reason for the relative absence of ethnic irredenta is the processes of integration that occurred in the colonial and postcolonial periods and that weakened the emotional-ethnic ties to such an extent that the different sections of the partitioned groups developed differential interests, feelings, and identities. Their exposure to different administrations, educational systems, colonial languages, markets, currencies, economic policies, mass media, and political orientations quite often led to the emergence of different identities. Some examples of these processes of gradual estrangement were researched by Miles, Morton, and Vail who studied the Hausas of Nigeria and Niger,[29] the Bakgatla baga Kgafela of Botswana and South Africa,[30] and the "Swazi" of Swaziland and South Africa,[31] respectively. Sometimes different names were given to the various parts of the divided groups (e.g., the Yoruba of Nigeria are called Nago in Benin, the Toubou of Chad are Goranes in Niger, and the Liberian Kpelle are known as Guerze in Guinea).

The surprising paucity of irredenta in Africa is partly due to the plural "softness" of the African postcolonial state. In most states the central government has neither the will nor the capacity to turn "Jacobin"—to force the partitioned and peripheral groups to assimilate, to conform, or to adapt to the center. Most states are plural, multiethnic states, which have developed informal mechanisms to make life at least bearable for most ethnic groups. This adjustment is made easier by the fact that the postcolonial state is not a nation-state in which the partitioned group is the only minority. The state is a state of minorities, and a group that is left out of power and its amenities is more likely to seek redress within the same state than to look for salvation across the border. The softness of the African state also means that partitioned groups may ignore the border at will. Such a liberal partition mitigates their "unhappiness" and diminishes the pressure on "their" government to adopt an irredentist policy on their behalf.

Realpolitik and utilitarian calculations by the potentially redeeming states are the major reasons for the relatively small number of African irredenta and their failure to change the postcolonial map dramatically. The multiethnic character of most African states and their internal lack of cohesion and stability are the prime reasons for their unwillingness to go irredentist, as they could easily fall victim to irredentist retaliation. Suhrke and Noble rightly claim that the feelings of vulnerability of the multiethnic states "lead to a restrained policy toward boundary disputes,"[32] and irredentism is certainly a kind of boundary dispute. A state that has to worry about lack of cohesion and possible disintegration will indeed act according to a "calculus of vulnerability."[33] It will hesitate to support irredentism in another state when this could serve as a precedent for irredentism within its own borders.   The Kenyan Masinde Muliro vividly evoked the fear of disintegration by irredentism when he rhetorically asked, "What would remain of Kenya if the Somalis unite with Somalia, the Luo and Abeluhya with their brothers in Uganda and the coastal Nyika and inland Masai break away to be together with their people in Tanzania?"[34]

Other "rational" calculations may dampen the enthusiasm for irredentism. Touval observed that "the delicate balancing of tribal interests in each state has apparently exercised a moderating influence, restraining governments from embracing open irredentist policies which might upset the existing tribal balance."[35] We should also bear in mind that "not all the ethnic constituents of such a state will be equally enthusiastic at the prospect of incurring costs and risks on behalf of the ethnic brethren of only one of them."[36]

The fear of destabilizing a delicate ethnic balance of power and the lack of any irredentist motivation by the other ethnic groups in the common state prevented Nigeria from adopting Ibo, Yoruba, and Hausa irredentist aspirations, mitigated Togolese irredentism after the mid-1960s, and accounted for the careful policies of bicommunal Djibouti vis-à-vis Greater Somalia and Greater Danakilia. The fellow countrymen of the Ibos, Yorubas, Hausas, Ewes, and Issas rationally opposed any ethnic irredentism that could strengthen their rivals within their states.

Another rationale for the state to stay away from irredentism is "the poor prospect of victory or its probable cost under the circumstances of a generalized war."[37] We have already mentioned that the ethnic brothers across the border may come to a similar realistic assessment of the situation. Sometimes both may grossly miscalculate and lose an all-out irredentist war, as did Somalia and the Western Somalia Liberation Front (WSLF) in 1977–1978.

Because "enthusiasm for 'redemption' of all but the most fervid ethno-secessionists is affected by cost/benefit expectations" and because "governments always make these calculations and take their decisions in the context of a prevailing interstate systemic environment as well as in the context of domestic political pressures, opportunities and risks,"[38] irredentism in Africa is relatively rare. Even in cases where the state would like irredentism to succeed, instrumental calculations will usually override ethnofraternal emotions and prevent the state from active involvement and commitment. Rothschild argues that the cases where utilitarian considerations reinforce ethnic irredentist aspirations are usually quite rare, and in all cases where the raison d'état is opposed to feelings of ethnic brotherhood, the potentially redeeming state will disappoint the irredentists.

The pursuit of irredentism also runs counter to the prevailing status quo ideology of the OAU and the African political establishment. Clause III of the OAU Charter (1963) talks about the obligation of the member states to respect "the sovereignty and territorial integrity of each state,"[39] and the Cairo Resolution of 1964 declares "the borders of the African states on the day of independence constituted a tangible reality" and that "the member states pledge themselves to respect the borders existing on their achievement of independence."[40] The OAU as an organization has indeed opposed all irredentist movements, and this consistent position, shared by most African governments, certainly strengthened the status quo forces in Africa and weakened the case for revisionism, whether separatist, irredentist, or expansive. Although Tolstoy's statement that divided peoples are unhappy is certainly true, in reality "the sword of self-determination is sharp when severing the colony from its metropole. However, its reverse side is blunt and unavailable when minorities within the former colonies seek either their own independent state or union with more desirable brothers across the frontier."[41]

NOTES

1. A. I. Asiwaju, "The Conceptual Framework," in A. I. Asiwaju, ed., *Partitioned Africans* (New York: St. Martin's Press, 1985), p. 2.

2. V. Matthies, *Der Grenzkonflikt Somalias mit Äthiopien und Kenya* (Hamburg: Insitut fur Afrikakunde, 1977), p. 73.

3. H. M. Adam, "Language, National Consciousness and Identity: The Somali Experience," in I. M. Lewis, ed., *Nationalism and Self-Determination in the Horn of Africa* (London: Ithaca Press, 1983), p. 31.

4. C. Legum, "Somali Liberation Songs," *Journal of Modern African Studies* 1, 4 (1963): 503–519.

5. *Africa Report* (May–June 1981): 12–14.

6. M. Pomerance, *Self-Determination in Law and Practice* (The Hague: M. Nijhoff, 1982), p. 12.

7. H. Macmillan, "A Nation Divided? The Swazi in Swaziland and Transvaal 1865–1986," in L. Vail, ed., *The Creation of Tribalism in Southern*

Africa (Berkeley: University of California Press, 1989), pp. 289–323.

8. B. Neuberger, *Involvement, Invasion and Withdrawal: Qadhdhafi's Libya and Chad* (Tel Aviv: Shiloah Center for Middle Eastern and African Studies, 1982), p. 47.

9. C. G. Widstrand, ed., *African Boundary Problems* (Uppsala: Scandinavian Institute of African Studies, 1969), p. 82.

10. C. Welch, *Dream of Unity: Pan-Africanism and Political Integration in West Africa* (Ithaca N. Y.: Cornell University Press, 1966), p. 142.

11. J. Damis, *Conflict in Northwest Africa: The Western Sahara Dispute* (Stanford, Calif.: Hoover Institution Press, 1983), p. 54; and T. Hodges, *Western Sahara: The Roots of a Desert War* (Brooklyn, N. Y.: Lawrence Hill, 1983), pp. 100–102.

12. R. Tholomier, *Djibouti: Pawn in the Horn of Africa* (Metuchen, N.J.: Scarecrow Press, 1981), p. 134.

13. B. Akinyemi, "Nigeria and Fernando Poo: The Politics of Irredentism," *African Affairs* 69, 276 (July 1970): 236–249; V. Levine, *The Cameroun Federal Republic* (Ithaca, N.Y.: Cornell University Press, 1971), p. 16; Z. Cervenka, *The Nigerian War 1967–1970* (Frankfurt: Bernard and Graefe, 1971), p. 70; and S. Touval, "The Sources of the Status-Quo and Irredentist Policies," in C. G. Widstrand, ed., *African Boundary Problems* (Uppsala: Scandinavian Institute of African Studies, 1969), pp. 106–109.

14. Matthies, *Der Grenzkonflikt Somalias*, pp. 10–11.

15. S. Healy, "The Changing Idiom of Self-Determination in the Horn of Africa," in I. M. Lewis, ed., *Nationalism and Self-Determination in the Horn of Africa* (London: Ithaca Press, 1983), p. 98.

16. *Ethiopia Observer*, September 16, 1966.

17. M. Reisman, "Somali Self-Determination in the Horn," in I. M. Lewis, ed., *Nationalism and Self-Determination in the Horn of Africa* (London: Ithaca Press, 1983), p. 153.

18. M. Wolde-Mariam, "The Background of the Ethno-Somalian Dispute," *Journal of Modern African Studies* 2, 2 (1964): 189–219, at p. 217.

19. Hodges, *Western Sahara*, pp. 85–91.

20. S. Touval, *Boundary Politics in Africa* (Cambridge, Mass.: Harvard University Press, 1972), p. 35.

21. Hodges, *Western Sahara*, pp. 25–36; and Damis, *Conflict in Northwest Africa*, pp. 11–12, 21–29.

22. L. Vail and L. White, "Tribalism in the Political History of Malawi," in Vail, *Creation of Tribalism in Southern Africa*, pp. 151–192; and S. H. Phiri, "The Chewa and Ngoni," in A. I. Asiwaju, ed., *Partitioned Africans* (New York: St. Martin's Press, 1985), pp. 105–125.

23. Welch, *Dream of Unity*, p. 200.

24. Ibid., p. 170.

25. Ibid., p. 211.

26. Phiri, "The Chewa and Ngoni," p. 117.

27. D. Horowitz, *Ethnic Groups in Conflict* (Berkeley: University of California Press, 1985), p. 282.

28. S. Touval, "Partitioned Groups and Inter-State Relations," in Asiwaju, *Partitioned Africans*, p. 223–232.

29. W. F. S. Miles, "Self-Identity, Ethnic Affinity and National Consciousness: An Example from Rural Hausaland," *Ethnic and Racial Studies* 9, 4 (October 1986): 427–444.

30. R. F. Morton, "The Bakgatla baga Kgafela of Bechuanaland," in Asiwaju, *Partitioned Africans*, pp. 127–154.

31. Macmillan, "A Nation Divided?" pp. 289–323.

32. A. Suhrke and L. G. Noble, eds., *Ethnic Conflict in International Relations* (New York: Praeger, 1977), p. 13.

33. Ibid., p. 17.

34. Matthies, *Der Grenzkonflikt Somalias*, pp. 244–245.

35. Touval, "Sources of the Status Quo," p. 69.

36. J. Rothschild, *Ethnopolitics: A Conceptual Framework* (New York: Columbia University Press, 1981), p. 183.

37. Suhrke and Noble, *Ethnic Conflict*, p. 17.

38. Rothschild, *Ethnopolitics*, pp. 182, 187.

39. S. Chime, "The Organisation of African Unity and African Boundaries," in C. G. Widstrand, ed., *African Boundary Problems* (Uppsala: Scandinavian Institute of African Studies, 1969), p. 66.

40. J. Mayall, "Self-Determination and the OAU," in I. M. Lewis, ed., *Nationalism and Self-Determination in the Horn of Africa*, p. 91.

41. R. Emerson, "The Problem of Identity, Selfhood and Image in New Nations, " *Comparative Politics* 1, 3 (April 1969): 297–312, at p. 300.

CHAPTER 8

Language Planning as an Aid and a Barrier to Irredentism

BRIAN WEINSTEIN

If a variety of language can be chosen, shaped, and promoted by cultural elites or governments and then accepted by the masses of people as the threatened symbol of a highly valued group identity and as the threatened legitimate instrument of their access to power, wealth, and prestige, then political elites should be able to recruit the same masses into a movement whose ostensible goal is the defense of that language. Under a linguistic banner, elites direct the mobilized people to support or to challenge the political, economic, or social structures that are perceived to accept or to reject users of the language. The same process of mobilization can serve elite efforts to create, alter, eliminate, or strengthen internal administrative boundaries or external international frontiers when those frontiers are perceived to be based on language differences and when they are perceived to affect pursuit of symbolic and tangible interests. In other words, language planning in a multilingual setting, where linguistic differences can be identified as regionally based ethnic or national differences, may be a useful instrument for leaders of irredentist and secessionist movements; and it should be equally useful for the opponents of irredentist and secessionist movements.

What is language planning? Who are the cultural elites who use it to transform a variety of language into a symbol of valued identity and a good instrument of interest satisfaction? How do they work with political elites to create a language movement whose ultimate goal is the detachment of a people and their land from one state and their unification with a neighboring state? How do others use language planning to prevent such a change in frontiers? What can one learn about irredentism and language planning from the examples of Kosovo, Macedonia, Alsace, and elsewhere?

LANGUAGE CHANGE AND LANGUAGE PLANNING

A language's form and function change gradually and imperceptibly to suit the evolving interests and preferences of its users. In other words,

111

there is a communication marketplace in all human societies. Without the intervention of any authority, speakers abandon certain written and spoken forms and they adopt others; they decide it is useful to learn a new language or even to invent a means of communication such as a pidgin for new needs, such as trade. Market forces easily change the spoken language. Written languages change more slowly.

Conscious, organized efforts are required to alter the form and the function of a written language because of the economic, status, and ideological interests of the literary producers, such as scribes, printers, and writers, and because of the economic, political, and ideological interests of institutional consumers, such as governments, businesses, and the clergy. The initiative for change is either from the individual producer or from an institution that then attempts to disseminate the innovations to others. Writers, teachers, journalists, linguists, and poets innovate by using a variety of written language for new purposes and by changing its form; to legitimize their choices they often call for institutional approval. In anticipation of resistance they are likely to organize themselves into pressure groups or into a language movement if they win mass support. The goal of concerted action is often to force authorities to select their favored variety of language as the medium of education and institutional business and as a symbol of the community. Language movements in Quebec and in India were part of a larger undertaking to transform the patterns of access to wealth, power, and prestige. Their success in making French and Tamil official media of government business and education helped middle-class, urban French-speakers and non-Brahmin, middle-caste Tamil-speakers to accede to high positions in the business sector and the government bureaucracy, and to gain a new self-respect.

If government or other important institutions respond to these pressures, or if they take the initiative themselves by making a policy choice and then implementing it, they are planning. In a country like France, there are many examples of planning from government initiatives and of planning as a government response to pressures. In 1539, the Villers-Cotterets decree required the judicial system of France to use the French language. In 1975, partly in response to calls for action, the Bas-Lauriol law was approved; it prohibited foreign terms in advertising when an acceptable French term already existed. The creation of new acceptable French terms to replace "Americanisms" is an outcome of that recent legislation, and failure to use them is punishable under laws defining fraud. Thus, language-planning activity can be defined as the choice of language form or choice of domain of usage made by important institutions capable of implementation over a significant area or among a significant population. Most of these institutions enjoy the implicit or explicit sanction of the state, but it is important to underline the fact that the original impulse for an institution's action is often the work of individual creative writers and their supporters. This will be evident in the chapter.

Institutions choose and implement language forms because they perceive that their interests will be served by changing the form and function of a language. These interests include facilitating communication for its own sake by standardizing or simplifying orthography, for example. Most often they involve altering or reinforcing patterns of access to desired values and transforming the identity of the society through language as a symbol. Language policy choices and planning must satisfy some nonlinguistic interest to be effective; language planning is one of many instruments for reaching ideological, economic, political, or social goals, but because the manifest goals and choices are linguistic, these interests may be masked.

The distinction between government-initiated planning and planning as a result of an organized nongovernmental effort is significant, particularly for the study of irredentism. Governments may be unable to make explicit language choices because of the fear of a reaction from other governments that perceive the action to be threatening; or they may hesitate out of fear of the uncontrollable internal consequences, including the reaction of groups within a heterogeneous society that do not use the language. As a result, a sympathetic government may prefer that writers and nongovernmental organizations try to initiate change without government intervention. In other situations, particularly at the beginning stages of a secessionist movement, no government exists to sanction the writers' choices. It will be only after secession and unification with a neighboring state that a government will be able to officialize the choices. In this case, writers and nongovernmental organizations have total responsibility for innovation.

The distinction and possible link between irredentism and secession are also significant in understanding the process and goals of language planning. The independence of Bangladesh, which was initiated by a nongovernmental language movement led by writers and other intellectuals, is an example of secession. The separation of the Bengali-speaking population living in East Pakistan from the rest of Pakistan satisfied the interests of that population, as far as one can tell. There were no significant calls for unity with India. India, with a large and contiguous Bengali population, did not work for the attachment of the new state to India. Thus, secession can take place without irredentism, but irredentism is greatly helped by secessionist sentiments. Irredentism may be defined as a "decision to retrieve group members across a territorial border by forcibly altering the border [and] is a governmental decision."[1] A secessionist movement among the target community can only strengthen irredentism. As Jacob Landau shows in

Chapter 6, secessionists may precede irredentists. If there is no secessionist movement among a target population echoing the claims of the
retrieving irredentist state, the latter is likely to be accused of engaging
in pure expansionism or imperialism. Without secessionist sentiments,
it will be more difficult for a retrieving state to claim it is working to
help an oppressed kin group or to claim it is promoting universally
accepted values such as religious freedom, cultural identity, and so
forth. What is pure expansionism in one century can be transformed
into irredentism in another century if the ethnic identity of the target
population has changed through language planning. Thus, as we shall
see, the annexation of Alsace by France in the seventeenth century was
an example of imperial expansion without regard to the identity of the
population. The demand for the return of the same territory to France
after World War I was irredentist because of the change in the identity
of the population, achieved partly through language planning.

The language choices that can sharpen or alter a sense of identity
are of two general types: corpus and status. Corpus planning, a term introduced by Heinz Kloss, is a change in the visible and audible form of
the language—what script is used, how words are spelled, which dialect
will serve as the standard, what neologisms to accept. Status planning,
according to Kloss, is the implementation of the decision to use a
particular variety of language for new functions—to write the laws of
the country, as a medium of instruction, and which dialect or variety
will serve as the standard. An example of status planning is declaring
Bahasa the medium of government business and education in Indonesia
and Malaysia. Bilingual education in the United States, which provides
for instruction through the medium of Spanish alongside English, is
another example. Examples of corpus planning are the changes in the
spelling of American English initiated by Noah Webster and adopted by
schools and the U. S. Government Printing Office; the creation of
neologisms by Academy of the Hebrew Language; and the reduction to
writing of Slavic tongues begun by the missionaries Cyril and Methodius
a thousand years ago and accepted by the Orthodox church.

Each form of planning serves symbolic and instrumental purposes.
Choice of one written form as the standard for all people who consider
themselves members of an ethnic group or nation can serve as a symbol
of their unity and as an instrument of important communication. They
may not, in fact, be able to write this language because they are
illiterate or because it is very different from their own variety of the
language. They may not even be able to understand the literary language when it is spoken. Inability to understand Koranic Arabic or
literary Tamil, even when they are spoken, does not lessen loyalty to
and pride in these languages among Moroccans and South Indians,
although it might do so if class differences were perceived as identical

with language differences. The persistence of differences between the language chosen and accepted as a symbol of identity and the variety of language actually understood by the majority of people gives an immense advantage to cultural elites in the short run: they are able to manipulate the language freely. In the long run, however, they risk being accused of pursuing their own narrow class interests in the guise of ethnic secession or irredentism. Successful introduction of their class-based variety of language into the schools may also result in blocking generations of lower-class students who are unable to master the new standard for which they fought during a secessionist or irredentist movement. In the long run, it may become obvious that the standard form chosen by the elites has given an advantage to persons who know the language as a mother tongue. They identify themselves as closest to the norms of the community, and they enjoy easiest access to attractive positions. Disappointments with the results of one irredentist movement could encourage another and opposing movement.

Throughout history one can find examples of language choice affecting political identities. Officialization of Turkish spoken in Istanbul and written in the Roman script encouraged development of a particular Turkish identity and discouraged written communication and identification with Muslim Arabic-using countries. Promotion of French and suppression of Breton in France and Wolof in Senegal through the education system helped to unify the peoples of France and then to link French elites with educated elites in France's African colonies. Teaching through the medium of Swahili has helped unite Tanzanians socially and ethnically and has served as a symbol of nationhood and freedom from the German and British colonial pasts. In this way, language is manipulated through planning to affect feelings of identity and to facilitate or bar communication among people who are alternately described as belonging or not belonging together in one political community. Creation of an identity or reinforcement of an identity through the actions of cultural elites is an important prerequisite to secessionist, irredentist claims as well as to their opponents.

ELITES AND LANGUAGE PLANNING

Nongovernmental cultural elites who initiate language planning are likely to belong to strata of language communities most affected by technological, socioeconomic, and political changes that produce new professions, new classes, and other groups whose interests are not satisfied by existing structures. Blockage of the ambitions of intellectuals emerging out of newly urbanized middle classes, or of the ambitions of intellectuals absorbed into a new state structure after annexation, can force demands for change. In Quebec, urbanization, industrialization, and expansion of education produced new demands from a French-speaking population newly conscious and angry about the disparities between their income potential and status and that of Anglophones. Through their writings an emerging group of urbanized middle-class Francophones demanded change, including officialization of the French language, which would facilitate their economic mobility. Political elites called for new parties and secession as the best way to realize these demands. The all-India independence movement, with its expansion of education, urbanization, and indigenization of the civil service, increased the numbers of non-Brahmin aspirants to urban, government, and university positions in South India. These Tamils promoted their language as weapons against the Sanskrit-using Brahmins and English-using colonizers, who monopolized the best positions and considered themselves at the high end of the scale of regard.

Tracing the initiatives of cultural elites such as writers, poets, singers, dictionary makers, and others through their publications is not difficult. It is also possible to trace the diffusion of their linguistic innovations through their networks of colleagues and friends to school teachers and local opinion leaders who have direct contact with the masses. Resistance can also be observed. Intellectuals who introduce innovations of form into their languages for political purposes have been called "language strategists."[2] Their suggestions about language are made with an eye on change in identity or eventual frontier alteration to conform with the language community. Noah Webster clearly stated that one reason for spelling a word "labor" instead of "labour" was to help build a symbol that would both unify the people of the United States and differentiate them from the people of England. He wrote in 1789: "Let us then seize the present moment and establish a *national language*, as well as a national government."[3]

Biographies reveal the network links between the writers and political leaders or aspiring political leaders. Noah Webster knew Benjamin Franklin and corresponded with John Adams; he had studied at Yale during the revolutionary period and met men who were to be important in Connecticut politics and university life. He attempted to promote his linguistic innovations among them, but was unsuccessful in urging the government to sanction all his choices. When political elites made clear to him that it was not in the long-term interest of the United States to cut all links with the former mother country, Webster revised his most radical suggestions for spelling change.

Acceptance of the close ties between American and British English or English and Latin influences the development of the corpus of American English. All languages must be enriched with new words to fit new phenomena. Writers may search in the old literary works for such words, especially if there is such a storehouse as there is for Greek and Hebrew. They may search in related languages or in unrelated languages considered politically neutral. U. S. scientists regularly turn to Latin and Greek to create neologisms without fear of political subordination. French intellectuals and planners concerned about U. S. cultural influence prefer to create new French words, to use old French words in new ways, or to translate in order to replace Americanisms. Accepting foreign words is one way of accepting and even legitimizing political and cultural proximity.   Refusal to borrow from certain languages or an effort to purify the language of borrowed words is part of an effort to create political distance. In the view of some of the most militant proponents of French purism, borrowing from American English means language servitude, and "language servitude leads inexorably to political and cultural servitude."[4] Promotion of the Russian language and promotion of Russian neologisms in non-Russian languages are part of an effort to spread universal knowledge of that language in the Soviet Union as one means to unite diverse peoples and weaken local nationalisms, some of which could serve irredentist claims from surrounding states.

LANGUAGE PLANNING AND IRREDENTISM

Efforts to sharpen or to change identities through language planning can be part of an irredentist policy and a related secessionist movement. In the early stages of such movements, language choices have awakened or sharpened mass sentiments of identity and solidarity across national political frontiers by creating a symbol of nationhood or shared nationhood in disharmony with current political frontiers. Promotion of one literary language has then facilitated communication among these people, who are then able to share more experiences and a sense of common nationhood. If retrieval takes place, language planning can serve to consolidate boundary changes and to prevent future irredentist claims from the state that lost the territory and population.

There are also examples of language planning designed to discourage or block irredentism and secession. Changing a language and emphasizing differences between one population and another discourage effective solidarity and effective communication. The masses are led to believe they are basically different from people across the frontier with whom they were perhaps once united. Latent irredentism may be defused by the willingness of two states to facilitate cooperation in language planning between members of an ethnic group living on both sides of the frontier. The desires for symbolic solidarity and effective communication are satisfied—at least for the time being—without altering frontiers or transferring populations. Flemish-speakers in Belgium and the Netherlands help maintain a variety of their language in northern France. Despite the unreality of any irredentist claims under present circumstances, the French educational authorities at first tried to discourage any recognition of Flemish. When it was decided to introduce regional languages into French schools as subjects of limited study, Flemish and Alsatian were excluded because they were considered foreign languages, unlike Breton. Limited Flemish instruction is now permitted, and Belgians, in particular, encourage their French Flemish kin to learn the standard Dutch spelling through essay contests and other activities.[5] Similarly, the Dutch and Belgian Flemish cooperate on language planning to ensure some common development of their varieties of language.

On September 9, 1980, the central government of Belgium and the government of the Netherlands signed a convention on the Union of the Dutch Language, Nederlands Taalunie. This is the basis of transnational planning similar to the work on Bahasa Indonesia and Bahasa Malaysia. The agreement's authors explained that cooperative planning was necessary to maintain a standard and that the planning that required joint organizations would not be a threat to the integrity of either Belgium or the Netherlands. The Belgian government declared that it considered "anything affecting the Dutch language [to be] the shared concern of the two countries and neither one could claim precedence."[6] Specifically, the agreement provides for the creation of joint language planning agencies to set a common spelling and grammar and to ensure that there is no divergence in official terminologies.[7]

Language planning in Kosovo, Macedonia, Alsace, and Moldavia/Bessarabia is very different from the Dutch-Flemish examples. The work of writers and institutions reflects and promotes irredentist feelings or efforts to suppress those feelings. Corpus and status planning are also closely linked with interstate conflict, which is in part the result of disagreements concerning the fate of ethnic groups living on both sides of international frontiers.

Kosovo

Albanian-speaking Yugoslavs living in the Autonomous Socialist Province of Kosovo are a contemporary example of secession related to irredentism. It is true that the most explicit calls for change are for separate republican status within Yugoslavia to replace the present incorporation within the Serbian republic. Some observers think that secession and unity with Albania are the true goals of demonstrators and elites in Kosovo. Language planning has assisted this effort by pulling Albanian Yugoslavs closer to Albania and further away from their Serbian neighbors. The government of Albania hesitates to make explicit irredentist claims on Kosovo because of the risks of confrontation with much larger and more powerful Yugoslavia and possibly because they are not completely sure how the annexation of a million people would affect their own political system. Nevertheless, there are signs that some important leaders are looking forward to the creation of a Greater Albania as the final and attainable goal of a nationalist movement that is one hundred years old. In other words, Hedva Ben-Israel's view of irredentism as a "phase of nationalism" in Chapter 2 probably fits the Albanian case.

The Autonomous Socialist Province of Kosovo, contiguous with northern Albania, has an area of 4,127 square miles with "a population of over a million and a quarter, of whom approximately three-fourths (73.8%) or nearly one million . . . are Albanians."[8] Since the beginning of a recent and concerted effort to drive out the Serbs, it is not unlikely that the Albanian dominance in the province has reached 80 percent. Adding to this group the Albanians in Macedonia and Montenegro, there are more than 1.3 million Albanians in Yugoslavia, or about one-third of all the Albanians in the world.

Both Serbs and Albanians have a sincere emotional attachment to the lands of Kosovo. The former refer to Kosovo as Old Serbia; it has served as a focus for Serbian identity. The "medieval Serbian kings were crowned there," and in the fourteenth century "the Serbian bishopric of Pec in Kosovo was proclaimed a patriarchate, thus making the Serbian church independent of the patriarch of Constantinople."[9] The Turks defeated the Serbs in a historic, decisive battle at Kosovo in 1389, and the Serbs vowed to retake Kosovo. After this conquest the Christian Serbs moved north into Hungary, and the Islamized Albanians moved in.

Albanians claim an earlier settlement as Illyrians, but documentation for that claim is less sure. What is certain is that a modern Albanian identity and sense of unity began to form in the Kosovo area. The desire for an independent nation-state crystallized at Kosovo in the late nineteenth century "and the armed struggle against the Turks in 1909–1912 [was] predominantly the work of the Albanians of Kosovo."[10] No matter who was first, Kosovo will always be important for both Serbians and Albanians.

During the collapse of the Ottoman Empire after World War I and the great-power negotiations about the boundaries of the newly created states in the Balkans, Kosovo was attached to Serbia and Serbians were encouraged to return there. According to some accounts, lands were seized from Albanians for the benefit of the Serbs, and Albanian resistance was brutally suppressed.[11] Thousands of Albanians emigrated from Kosovo into Turkey and Albania, including the family of the current president of Albania, Ramiz Alia. Some of these emigrants probably urged the interwar Albanian government to make irredentist claims on Kosovo.

Germans and Italians occupying Yugoslavia and Albania in World War II changed the frontiers again. Much of Kosovo was annexed to Albania, and in gratitude "most of the quislings and supporters of the Italian regime were Albanians from Kosovë or from northern Albania."[12] Communists of Yugoslavia and Albania cooperated in fighting against the Fascists. The Yugoslav Communist party had declared in 1928 and in 1940 that "Kosovo should be restored to Albania."[13] Before the invaders were driven out, the Albanian Communist leadership called for self-determination of the Kosovo population. In September 1943, Enver Hoxha said:

> The national liberation movement has the task of making the Kosovë people conscious of their aspirations, and they will succeed in liberating themselves. . . . We must see that the people of Kosovë decide for themselves which side to join . . . and to oppose the Yugoslav regime which would attempt to oppress them.[14]

The wartime National Liberation Committee for Kosovë and Metohija resolved that after the war "all the nations, including the Albanians, will be able to choose their own destiny, with the right to self-determination—including secession."[15]

Yugoslav leader Josip Broz Tito promised the Albanians equality and resolution of the earlier-mentioned land problems. Perhaps that was the reason the National Liberation Committee passed a resolution that Kosovo be reunited with the Republic of Serbia within a new Socialist Yugoslavia.[16] However, it is difficult to believe that the vote was free and by a representative body because in the countryside there was a fierce armed resistance to the returning Yugoslav authorities "until March 1945," according to Prifti.[17] During the four decades after the end of World War II, Albanians have claimed that the old patterns of discrimination against them have not abated, and despite investments by the central government the gross national product of Kosovo has remained very low. Kosovo has kept its unenviable reputation as the most backward area of Yugoslavia, and the ability of the central government to invest funds there has declined, making matters worse.

Beginning in the late 1960s, the Kosovars experienced a freedom to resist Serb dominance, partly because of the disgrace of the famous centralizer, Aleksander Rankovic, in 1966; increased urbanization; the emergence of a significant group of students; and possibly help from the Albanian diaspora in North America and elsewhere. In November 1968, mass demonstrations shook Kosovo; the young crowds "carried Albanian flags and hailed Enver Hoxha; they also broke shop windows, especially those bearing Serbian inscriptions."[18] Demonstrators demanded the creation of an all-Albanian university, and the following year the University of Prishtina was established. Its faculty, which was quickly Albanianized, has articulated demands for political change, and some of the professors may be linked to the shadowy Revolutionary Movement of United Albania "which may have enjoyed Albania's support."[19] In 1971, constitutional amendments provided Kosovo with more self-rule, and that same year Yugoslavia and Albania normalized their diplomatic relations. Friendly relations between Belgrade and Tirana facilitated cultural exchanges. In 1981, rioting Albanians in Kosovo "demanded either republic status for Kosovo or outright secession."[20] From about 1984 to the present, attacks on individual Serb residents of Kosovo have begun to drive them out of the area. Demands for republic status are louder, but many observers believe the ultimate goal is unity with Albania. Serbs protesting the treatment received at the hands of Albanians were told as recently as March 1986 by Lazar Mojsov, member of the country's collegial presidency, that Yugoslav leaders "were aware of the unleashing of extremist Grand Albanian nationalism and irredentism and that they planned to take measures against it."[21]

The Albanian leaders in Tirana are careful in their references to Kosovo and to relations with Yugoslavia in general, and they claim they wish to improve relations with Belgrade. Nevertheless, they "placed blame on Belgrade for the deterioration, which was traced to the Kosovo problem and what Tirana terms 'harsh treatment of Albanians in Kosovo and Macedonia.'"[22] Some party members in Tirana may be less than enthusiastic about union with the Kosovars because of doubts concerning their kin's commitment to communist ideology. According to Prifti, the Kosovo political and cultural elites used communism only as an instrument to pursue nationalist goals. There is also the matter of the image of Kosovars as a somewhat rebellious mountain folk who would cause trouble even within a newly united Albania. Cultural differences, to be discussed below, may make Tirana hesitate.

Would the agitation on both sides of the frontier dissipate if Kosovo were granted full republic status? In other words, are the agitation for secession and the hints about irredentism rhetorical devices to force the Yugoslav state to devolve more power to Kosovo elites? Probably not. The forces pushing for frontier change would continue. Albanians outside the Balkans agitate for unity of all Albanians in what they hope will be a noncommunist state. Albanians probably also hope that increased ethnic tensions, particularly between Croats and Serbs, will destroy the Yugoslav state permitting a general realignment of frontiers in the Balkans. Agitators probably know that many Serbs would resist separating Kosovo from Serbia even if Kosovo were to remain part of Yugoslavia, and Serb resistance could serve as an excuse for the explicit call for secession. Changes in Tirana may also prove to promote overt irredentism. The death in 1985 of party leader Enver Hoxha opened the way for Ramiz Alia, whose family, as indicated above, migrated from Yugoslavia into Albania in 1922[23] during a time of reported Serbian exactions against the Albanians. Furthermore, Ramiz Alia has a reputation for having supported the Fascist call for a greater Albania during World War II.[24] Symbolic gestures on behalf of Kosovo are widely reported:

> The post-Hoxha leadership has made it clear that it will continue to demand better treatment for the Albanian minority in Yugoslavia and will function as the center of Albanian nationalism. Symbolic of this attitude was the placement of an Albanian flag "on the heart of Enver on behalf of the Albanians of Kosovo before his coffin was lowered in the ground by his widow, Nexhmije."[25]

From the beginnings of the Albanians' search for national unity and independence, language has been an issue, and language planning has been an instrument of those trying to bring about secession and irredentism in contemporary times. Unlike Serbo-Croatian and Macedonian, the Albanian language is not a Slavic tongue, and, in fact, "is thought to stand in no close genealogical relationship with any other Indo-European language group."[26] (Thus, if one takes the translation of "Yugoslavia" literally—land of the South Slavs—the Albanians are excluded by definition.) Their standard literary language was chosen only after World War II, which makes Albanians very sensitive about its form and status.

During Ottoman times, few Albanians were literate, and those who could read and write did so through Turkish and Arabic if they were Muslim, or through Greek if they were Orthodox Christians. Students were divided according to faith, the literary language they studied in schools, and by alphabet. The Albanian language with its two major spoken varieties or dialects, Geg in the north and Tosk in the south, had no written standard and was disdained partly for that reason. Networks of intellectuals and nationalists formed in the several clubs set up near the end of Ottoman rule; they spread the idea that independent Albanian schools should be established and that they should either use Albanian as a medium of instruction or teach Albanian as a subject. With help coming from the Albanian diaspora, a few schools were created, and in 1908 the Ottoman government allowed the official teaching of Albanian.[27] Most of the ideas and pressures for language planning were coming from nongovernmental sources such as writers and teachers.

The first planning problem was selection of a standard written form that could serve as a medium of instruction in the schools. At that time, Albanian was written in Roman and Arabic. The Albanian club of Monastir invited members of other clubs to an "alphabet congress," held November 14–22, 1908. Three hundred persons attended, representing all Albanian communities including that in the United States, so that different religions and regions, in which different dialects were spoken, were encompassed.[28] Speakers of the Geg variety coming from the north, including Kosovo, tended to favor the Arabic alphabet; speakers of the Tosk variety coming from the south tended to favor the Roman alphabet.[29] Gegs were and are the definite majority of all Albanian speakers, and they dominate the Kosovo area and the mountains of northern Albania, but the Tosks from the southern lowlands felt self-confident about their dialect because of their generally higher level of education and ties with the Albanian diaspora. Fearing that dialect differences might preclude a united front of Albanian cultural and political elites, the 1908 congress delegates continually stressed the absolute necessity for Albanian unity no matter what.[30] Consequently they decided at first that students must learn both Roman and Arabic scripts.[31] Some Muslims opposed this rather reasonable solution, and the alphabet matter was left to the discretion of each school.

Another congress was held at Elbasan on September 2, 1909, to set up a normal school whose graduates would be sent to teach in the various new Albanian schools. Delegates grappled with the issue of a standard language for the schools to use. They proposed the central dialect of Elbasan, between north and south, "as it was intelligible to both Gegs and the Tosks."[32] They further proposed that the normal school should teach Albanian through the Roman script. Many Muslims opposed this choice, and there were demonstrations for and against, with Turkish and religious authorities supporting the use of Arabic script. Istanbul then ordered the closing of the schools and the suppression of the clubs, and the standardization issue remained unresolved for almost forty years.

After the attachment of Kosovo to Yugoslavia, the Albanian language was still suppressed, but this time by Serbs who feared Albanian national feeling. Promotion of Serbo-Croatian was Belgrade-directed status planning. Albanian-language schools were forbidden, and Serbo-Croatian was the only language used by government officials and teachers. Albanian, however, served as the language of instruction in a religious academy, the Great Medrese of King Aleksandar, set up to train Muslim imams. According to Blanc, the academy "became a center of nationalist and even Communist activity." Albanian-language books were brought in illegally from Albania.[33] Some of these books must have come from exiles who had settled in Albania and had formed the KK, or Committee for the National Defense of Kosovo.[34]

Using Albania as a base of operations, the KK launched occasional raids on Serbs across the border. Kosovo natives living in Albania also tried to influence local politics there, and they tried to overthrow the prime minister and future king, Ahmet Bej Zog, who was unfriendly to Kosovars. Gegs within Albania tended to support Zog, a northerner like themselves, whereas Tosks opposed him.[35] Zog suppressed the KK and maintained good relations with the noncommunist Serbs across the frontier.[36]

The Albanian language began to thrive during the Italian occupation. Kosovo opened new schools where students studied through their mother tongue. The Communists who opposed Italian rule also began to use Albanian in their underground literature, and to avoid dialect problems they carefully printed their pamphlets and posters in both the Geg and Tosk varieties,[37] even though party leaders were overwhelmingly Tosk.

After the end of the war, Albanian medium schools opened in Kosovo, but Serbo-Croatian was the language of the administration at least until 1968, when the province began to enjoy more autonomy. Bilingualism is essential for educated Albanians who wish to succeed in Yugoslavia, but it has not been necessary for their Serb neighbors. Janet Byron, a leading Albanologist, believes this pressure to use Serbo-Croatian has been a constant source of "frustration" for intellectuals keen on promoting Albanian.[38] In the absence of an official language planning agency or university, intellectuals, writers, and teachers met in 1952 to decide how to develop the corpus of the language and to improve its status. Belgrade approved their activities and must have been pleased that they decided on the principle "write what we speak."[39] This phrase meant that Geg would serve as a written standard, but basic books still had to be published and schools built for a population about 90 percent illiterate. Meanwhile, the government and party of Enver Hoxha chose the Tosk variety of Albanian as their standard, even though Tirana, the capital and most important city, is in Geg-speaking country. Byron has shown that only six out of the twenty-seven top Communist party leaders spoke Geg, and this fact must have been decisive in the choice of Tosk, but since the two varieties are mutually intelligible, Geg speakers would not be excluded from party deliberations.[40] In 1964, the Yugoslav Albanian writers published a Geg orthography and an anthology of Geg-Albanian literature,[41] which seemed to mean that they accepted two standards for Albanian. If so, that would tend to reinforce the political differences between Yugoslav and Albanian speakers of Albanian. Meanwhile, the Tosks were producing a much larger body of literature.

Between 1964 and 1968, a radical change took place in the thinking of writers. A few months before the explosions of anti-Serb and anti-

Yugoslav feeling in November 1968, a conference in Prishtina attended by journalists, intellectuals, and teachers abruptly proposed switching the standard literary form from Geg to Tosk. The participants suggested that the book of spelling rules published in Tirana the previous year be used as a guide (when planners in Tirana altered their own rules shortly thereafter, Yugoslav Albanians quickly followed).[42] Perhaps the desire to use Tosk had always been in the minds of Kosovars, but out of fear of Rankovic they chose Geg; or perhaps they were convinced to use Tosk by the example of literary production in Tirana. Whatever the specific reason for the shift in 1968, the general motive was an assertion of Albanian nationalism. As one enthusiastic Kosovo supporter of Tosk is reported to have said, "At present, the national Albanian language which the mother country uses has become imperative for all Albanians, wherever they live, all the more so because every national entity has only one standard language."[43] Despite the expense involved, Albanian publishers in Kosovo conformed to the new rules of spelling when they reprinted old works, originally written in Geg, in the newly chosen Tosk. Such a project is not easy or cheap, but the high rate of illiteracy in Kosovo facilitated the work, as the new literates did not have to unlearn one system of writing. They did, however, have to learn to write a language that was somewhat different from their mother tongue.

From 1969, the University of Prishtina and the Institute for Albanology served to institutionalize the language planning begun by writers and intellectuals. The Department of Albanian at the university has played a particularly important role in the planning of language and the agitation for political change. The existence of the university facilitates exchanges with the University of Tirana across the border. Yugoslavs traveled south, and books traveled north. Yugoslav professors and students perfected their Tosk-Albanian, and publishers carefully copied the forms they saw in Albanian publications. One interesting exception was the publication of a dictionary in Tirana in 1980 in which terms referring to Yugoslav institutions and variety of socialism were defined in very pejorative ways. Kosovo intellectuals and publishers carefully excised these terms or the negative definitions from the Kosovo edition of the dictionary.[44] They may have feared Yugoslav reactions, or perhaps the Kosovars did not agree with their Albanian cousins. If the latter is the correct explanation, it suggests some reservations about the Albanian political system.

Now, newspapers receive guidelines from the language planning agencies. Programs on radio and television are designed to help children speak as well as write Tosk. Special normative newspaper columns advise Kosovars how to improve their Tosk. In Byron's view, the promotion of Tosk for the last twenty years has built a firm constituency in Yugoslavia for this literary language.[45] After the riots of 1981, which began at the university, and until the present, exchanges of people and books between the two Albanian regions have been limited. Many of the most active promoters of cooperation have been dismissed from their university positions and from jobs at the radio and television stations.[46]

Shared language has been a convenient instrument and symbol of this movement, but it is not the only method of promoting Albanian secession and irredentism: "In Macedonia . . . Muslim clergy of Albanian extraction had exerted pressure on Macedonian Gypsies and Turks and on Muslim Macedonians, during a census taken early [in 1982] to declare themselves Albanians."[47] In fact, many of the Muslims of Macedonia are Albanians by tradition and language, and it is likely that Albania is watching events in that Yugoslav republic carefully.

Another nonlinguist force maintains the urge to unity. The present border between Yugoslavia and Albania has split up clans, the traditional organization of the Gegs. The clan, or *fis,* has been the focus of identity and order for northern mountain-dwelling Albanians over the centuries. Clan identity dictated marriage ties and other relationships. One or more clans living in the same area were united into a *bajrak* headed by a *bajraktar.*[48] Marmullaku says that Gegs are intensely loyal to these traditional organizations, out of which developed blood feuds and vendettas known elsewhere in the general area of the Mediterranean: "Among the Albanians in Yugoslavia the number of crimes committed in vendettas was rising until recently. Between 1964 and 1970, for instance, the circuit court in Prishtiné tried 320 cases involving blood feuds."[49] Such intra-Albanian conflicts contribute to the general atmosphere of tension in Kosovo. It may be that Gegs believe clan unification, a result of secession and then unity with Albania, will help them resolve clan disputes. It may be that the clan of Ramiz Alia is one that supports unification, but there is no way of knowing. Visitors to the area in 1990 report seeing public meetings during which feuds have been resolved and peace restored.

The issue of Kosovo will not soon abate. Experienced journalists, such as Henry Kamm of the *New York Times,* accept claims that Albania's "hostility to Yugoslavia has grown."[50] Tosk concerns about possible Geg domination are probably not, according to Byron,[51] a significant factor because Gegs already outnumber Tosks in Albania. Leaders on both sides of the frontier downplay differences and emphasize unity. In 1982, Enver Hoxha was reported to have said that "Albania was not a state of three million people but a nation of six million."[52] Language planning will continue to sharpen the Albanian sense of identity. Serbo-Croatian words are being removed by the planners; products are now labeled in Tosk; Tosk is used in Kosovo to subtitle foreign films and the use of Tosk in all media is taken for granted.

Although Byron does not believe that Yugoslav Albanians will all speak Tosk, they will read and understand it while speaking a distinct Yugoslav variant, much like the educated Quebec French.[53]

Macedonia

Language planning has been an even more important factor in efforts to create and maintain a Macedonian identity that could block irredentist claims by the Bulgarians. Before World War II, Serbians claimed that Macedonian was a dialect of Serbian, and Bulgarians appear still to believe that it is a dialect of Bulgarian. Before there was a Macedonian government, individual writers, intellectuals, and other members of the cultural elite fashioned a literary standard out of spoken dialects that were the most different from neighboring Bulgarian and Serbo-Croatian. The standard created out of corpus work provided a basis for the claim for a separate, well-defined identity meriting a distinct political entity in a liberated Yugoslavia. Macedonian was declared the official language of the Macedonian republic in 1944. After this status decision, planning for the corpus was institutionalized within the Department of Macedonian of the University of Skopje in 1946 and in the Misirkov Institute for the Macedonian Language in 1953.[54] The institute enriched the body of the language by publishing the first volume of a purely Macedonian dictionary in 1961, and other volumes followed in the next few years. The literary language, in the view of a leading intellectual, was "stabilized"; as such it now "offers a constant challenge to those who would like to ignore the fact of the political and cultural emancipation of a small nation."[55]

Bulgarians continue to refuse to recognize Macedonian identity and make irredentist claims that vary in intensity and openness depending on the warmth of their ties with Yugoslavia. During celebrations of the 1100th anniversary of the death of St. Methodius, who together with his brother Cyril reduced Slavic tongues to writing, Yugoslav authorities objected to Bulgarian claims that Methodius and Cyril were called Bulgarians instead of Macedonians.[56] Secession is not and has not been an issue here, but Macedonia is clearly a case of irredentism by Bulgaria. Corpus planning helped Macedonians officialize their language, thereby differentiating themselves from Serbs internally and from Bulgarians externally, and it helped raise an ideological barrier to irredentism.

Alsace

Status planning—the imposition of French, then German, then French as the sole medium of education and government business—has served as a barrier to irredentist claims on Alsace. Louis XIV seized this territory from the German Holy Roman Empire in 1648. A newly united Germany took it back after the Franco-Prussian War of 1870, the French regained control by 1918, the Germans took it in 1940, and it was returned to France by the end of World War II. Neither German nor French planners explicitly allowed for the official use of Alsatian, the tongue actually spoken by the people. They both tried to assimilate the population through French or German and to create a barrier to further irredentist demands from the state that had lost Alsace.

The first French annexation in 1648 was not, however, a case of irredentism. France's king saw this territory, which borders on the Rhine River, as important for the country's strategic defenses and economic development. Louis XIV knew how to make use of irredentist claims when it suited his purpose, as proven by the annexation of French-speaking Franche-Comté in 1688, but he could make no such claim for Alsace.[57]

After the annexation of Alsace, efforts began to assimilate the population through language planning, and thus to erect a barrier to future German irredentist claims, but quite late given the legendary French concern for their language. Members of the middle classes had been attracted to the splendor of French culture and regularly used the language of Paris,[58] but the vast majority spoke Germanic tongues. Although French was supposed to be the official language of all French territories, schools in Alsace continued to use the same German they had used before annexation. Churches used Alsatian, French, German, or Latin. Market forces supported German rather than French because most commerce was carried on with merchants across the Rhine, not west toward Paris. To discourage such business dealings, contracts written in German were declared invalid.[59] In 1661, Cardinal Mazarin created the Collège des Quatre Nations for sons of noble families in recently annexed regions. His purpose was to win their loyalty to the king and to France, but, interestingly, Mazarin did not think it important to require teachers to use the French language as the medium of instruction; consequently they used Latin.[60]

The nationalist ideology born during the French Revolution of 1789 made language much more important for national identity and loyalty. The dominant and centralizing Jacobins scorned German and Alsatian as well as Breton and other regional languages. During the war against Austria, France's republican rulers called the German language the symbol of the enemy; speaking German meant disloyalty to France. Thus, pressure to shift to French grew, and the government ordered teachers to teach through their language, not German. Because local teachers were more or less ignorant of French, the program was bound to fail. By the end of the eighteenth century, the only shift to French that had taken place was reportedly among the young Alsatians drafted into France's armies.[61]

Napoleon I, the kings who succeeded him, and Napoleon III accepted French-German bilingualism among their Alsatian subjects, despite strident irredentist calls coming from Germany. The absence of a dynamic assimilationist policy is a bit surprising because the Germans specifically raised the language issue in their claims, but it was not until the Third Republic that a very serious effort was made to promote French through the schools. Before 1870, the highest bureaucrats used French but town and village personnel used German. Market forces had shifted, however, and merchants then found it more profitable to know French than German. Some language planning promoted French in education: French was supposed to be the medium of instruction in secondary schools and universities from 1808 and in primary schools from 1853, according to Gutmann,[62] and the very first normal school in France was opened in Alsace in 1810. The graduates were supposed to be perfectly fluent in French; their duty was to spread French, but they were also taught German. However, signs that French had not spread very far were evident. In 1848, the major of Strasbourg publicly stated for the benefit of the German irredentists that even though Alsatians continued to use their language, they were loyal to France.[63] French writers, contradicting the ideology of the French Revolution—which the Germans found perfectly compatible with their claims on Alsace—denied that language defined the nation. Fustel de Coulanges and Renan asserted that nationhood was a matter of feeling and of love, a subjective feeling not necessarily dependent on language.

Alsatians were not asked about their sentiments in 1870 when a German victory forced reunification of Alsace with a newly united state. Berlin decreed German the official language of both Alsace and Lorraine. Towns using French were allowed to wait until 1878 to change to German.[64] The government also allowed the use of French in the courts and in primary schools in French-speaking areas. But street names, company names, and even family names were to be Germanized everywhere. At the beginning of World War I, pressure to conform intensified.

The French victory in 1918 automatically changed the official language in Alsace again. After almost fifty years of German rule, only 2 percent of the people were fluent in French and another 8 percent knew it "fairly well."[65] In order to integrate Alsace once and for all within the French nation and to prevent any further claims by Germans, the French formulated a language plan and implemented it in a heavy-handed and insensitive way. The highest-ranking administrators sent from Paris knew no German, forcing subordinates to learn French quickly; all written documents had to be in French, including public signs; and in schools French was to be the medium of instruction from the first day to the last. (In 1920, it was decided that some German would be used from the fourth year.) It is not surprising that, given the poor knowledge of French among Alsatian teachers and the arrogance of imported teachers, students were doing poorly, according to a study done in 1926. The system was reformed the following year with an allowance made for teachers to explain subjects in Alsatian when students did not understand French, but the language issue was politicized within Alsace when political parties took different stands on the question of the medium of instruction. In 1927, the Independent party of Alsace practically demanded independence.[66]

Between 1940 and 1945, the Nazis attempted to undo French works. Once again German became the language of the administration, the courts, and the schools. Within days of German control, street and shop names were changed. In 1941, according to Philipps, names on sink faucets within private homes were to be translated into German, and family names were changed. Tremendous pressure was put on people, particularly teachers, not to use French, a language of the enemy. Students in secondary schools were encouraged to study English rather than French as their first foreign language.[67]

The cycle resumed with the Allied victory, and "the teaching of German was completely banned in schools" until 1952 when it could be studied during "the last two years of school." In 1971, German language teaching was allowed for up to "half an hour a day" in secondary schools.[68] The socialist government that ruled from 1981 to March 1986 encouraged the study of what they called regional cultures and languages, and on September 23, 1985, Prime Minister Laurent Fabius created the National Council of Regional Languages and Cultures; but since the victory of the opposition in March 1986 the projects have been frozen.

In the present context of close and friendly ties between Germany and France, irredentist claims are inconceivable, but Gutmann contends in Chapter 3 that the region could be an eventual candidate for such claims. Language planning of a status nature was used to try to assimilate a German-speaking population into France, but French remains a second language, rather than the mother tongue, of most Alsatians. Although Alsatians do not speak and write standard German as a mother tongue, elites could attempt to promote loyalty to standard German in an effort to change frontiers, should the political and economic context change in a significant way. Language planning would be an important element in such circumstances.

Moldavia-Bessarabia

Similarly, unless there is a generalized true secession of Soviet republics,

Romania will not be able to retrieve Bessarabia or Moldavia within its national frontiers. The Soviet Union claimed to have reunited the Moldavian people with their kin within its borders after World War II, and the Russians are so much more powerful than the Romanians, whose new government is not so popular, that one might think they would not worry about any claims coming from Bucharest. In any case, elites in Romania and in what is called the Moldavian Soviet Socialist Republic (SSR) have succeeded in maintaining a viable Romanian identity through language planning. This became clear in 1989 and 1990 when frontier barriers were removed and freer movement was greeted with joy.

The first Russian annexation of Moldavia or Bessarabia in 1812 was similar to the first French annexation of Alsace. The rich land gave the czar an opportunity to increase food production and provided access to the Danube, the way possession of Alsace gave France access to the Rhine.[69] In 1856, part of Bessarabia was freed from Russian rule, but Turkey controlled Romanian-speaking areas. It was not until 1859 that Romania was created by the unification of Romanian-speaking principalities, but the Ottomans still ruled. The Romanians declared themselves independent in 1877, but they lost Bessarabia to the Russians in 1878 after the Russian defeat of Turkey.

In the confusion of World War I and the Russian Revolution, Bessarabian leaders declared their region independent and then united it with Romania. The Paris peace conference confirmed the unification after agreeing, on the basis of language, that Bessarabians were Romanians.[70] The Soviet Union refused to accept the decision and made open irredentist claims in the name of a very small kin population left within its borders. To provide a basis for future irredentist demands, the Soviets created the Moldavian Autonomous Republic (MAR) in 1924 out of a portion of the Ukraine contiguous with Romania. According to Bruchis, the MAR had never been part of the traditional principality of Moldavia, and the language spoken by the population was a heavily Ukrainized and Russified version of Romanian.[71] During World War II, the Soviet Union annexed Bessarabia once again, making it part of the MAR. Together they were transformed into the Moldavian SSR, whose population of 2.2 million was 90 percent Bessarabian.[72] This large disparity in population size—as well as the level of education and the quality of language used—would eventually have an important impact on language planning.

After the end of World War II, the Bucharest government and the Romanian Communist party hinted that they had claims on Bessarabia-Moldavia. The first generation of postwar Romanian leaders had been closely allied with Moscow, and Soviet troops were stationed in the country until 1958. With the advent to power of Ceauşescu in 1965, officially inspired nationalism intensified. The party leader's rhetoric was much more nationalistic than that of his predecessors; he regularly spoke of the need for *national* development and unity. Although this could be interpreted as one way to blunt criticism of his own policies within Romania, the references to nation and unity were also meant to refer to Bessarabia. In 1975, Ceauşescu said: "Historical experience teaches us that dismembering of some countries and the division of some nations has always been a break in the path of social development and hindered the peoples from mightily asserting their energies and creative capabilities in the fight for social progress, civilization and welfare."[73] The head of the party increased radio broadcasts in Romanian and about Romania toward the Soviet Union. By the 1970s, Bucharest published maps showing Bessarabia-Moldavia as part of Romania.[74] At a 1980 meeting of historians in Bucharest, what was called the Soviet occupation of Bessarabia was openly denounced.[75] On the Soviet side, Moldavians reportedly called openly for unity with Romania, but they were quickly jailed.[76] They are no longer jailed, but the changing political situation makes it difficult to predict future alignments and frontiers.

Cultural elites and language planning have served political decisions on each side of the frontier. Despite or because of Soviet attempts to create a new language out of the Ukrainized variety of Romanian spoken by some people in Moldavia as a way of building a barrier against eventual irredentist and secessionist demands, Romanian identity may have been sharpened among the educated.

Like Albanian and Macedonian, the standard literary Romanian is relatively recent. Although Romanian is a Romance language, it is surrounded by speakers of Slavic languages and, naturally, market forces dictate that speakers would borrow words and some syntactic forms from Slavic.[77] Early Romanian literature was also transcribed in the Cyrillic alphabet, giving an impression of Slavic identity. Writers began to search for a standard in the eighteenth century, and eventually they chose the spoken language of Bucharest, the most important city and later the capital of a united Romania.[78] The fact that Romania did not exist before 1877 delayed efforts to sanction the use of Romanian education and government. The use of Romanian as the official language of Romania fixed its status, and the creation of a Romanian academy facilitated corpus work. The academy produced the necessary dictionaries, grammars, and other books that enriched the language, and permitted use of the language in all domains of the society.[79] Purism seems to be part of the corpus planning, but this purism is politically inspired: Russian words are discouraged, and when borrowing is necessary the Romanian planners now prefer to depend on French.[80]

Feelings against the Russian language are strong: "Russian language . . . was dropped from schools, [and] the Russian Bookstore (*Cartea Rusa*) in Bucharest was demolished."[81]

On the Soviet side of the frontier, party officials and state-controlled cultural institutions have tried to use language planning to create a symbolic barrier between Moldavians and Romanians and to make communication difficult. Their main instrument was Ukrainized Romanian, which they tried to use as a standard language. Cultural elites within Moldavia have resisted this effort by insisting that their language is Romanian and then, through corpus work, keeping the literary language close to the Bucharest standard.

Although Moldavian officials have wanted to destroy Romanian identity, they allowed use of the language in education, unlike the czars who suppressed it. Russian is reportedly the language of government business, but Anderson and Silver believe that the bilingual education program is enough to prevent Russification, which some observers believe to be the very long term goal of Soviet cultural planning.[82] In 1980, there were only five exclusively Romanian high schools out of fifty-seven,[83] but it is doubtless true that there has been very little shift to Russian as a mother tongue.

Language planning is centralized in the Institute of Language and Literature of the Moldavian Academy of Science and the translations group of ATEM (The Telegraph Agency of Soviet Moldavia). These organizations are responsible to the central committee of the Moldavian Communist party. Under party orders, the linguists changed the name of the language to "Moldavian" and wrote it in the Cyrillic script instead of the Roman script in use in Bucharest. They attempted to use the spoken language of the old Moldavian Autonomous Republic as the standard, but this variety has no prestige and is not widely understandable. For many years an effort was made to exclude linguists and writers from the annexed areas from high positions in language planning agencies because they could not be trusted to avoid promoting the Bucharest standard.

Writers at the institute prepared spelling guides and dictionaries to promote Moldavian, and newspaper writers attempted to use it, but observers report that the results were disastrous. A very important Moldavian linguist and head of the institute, I. D. Cioban, who was born in the old MAR, published a Moldavian grammar, a speller, a Russian-Moldavian dictionary, and other books at the institute. He led the battle for separation from Romanian by claiming Moldavian was not even a Romance language, it was a Slavic tongue that naturally should borrow from Russian.[84] Writers outside the institute, particularly those from Bessarabia, published in the Bucharest variety, albeit in Cyrillic because it was against the law to publish in the Roman alphabet. A conflict grew, and Moscow feared that unexpected consequences from the acute antagonism between official planners and nongovernmental writers might threaten order. At a meeting called in 1951, Russian linguists from the prestigious USSR Academy of Sciences criticized Cioban who, not unexpectedly, was removed as director of the institute; they proclaimed that Moldavian was indeed a Romance language. Writers then felt freer to use the Bucharest standard.[85]

Probably to avoid controversy, while at the same time contributing to a sharpening of Romanian identity, many fiction writers began to publish works based on Romanian folklore. They also prepared translations of important novels and other literature into the standard Bucharest language. They strenuously tried to avoid Russian or Slavic words, even preferring to call the Soviet Union's 1957 Sputnik a *satelit*.[86] Such exaggerated purism is a sign of a siege mentality and recalls Quebec's refusal to use the word "stop" on traffic signs, although France accepts it. Inevitably, however, some words not in the Bucharest standard appeared, but the vigilant Romanian intellectuals added these Moldavian neologisms to their own "four-volume academic dictionary of modern literary Romanian which appeared in Romania in 1955–57."[87] Romanians were also sensitive to the views of disinterested parties. In April 1956, an Italian scholar in attendance at an international meeting in Florence proved that Moldavian and Romanian were one language. To show their appreciation, the Romanians gave him an honorary doctorate.[88] Because of the absence of many words in the Russified Romanian spoken in the old MAR, even ATEM, the official translation agency, tends to produce Bucharest-type works, according to Bruchis.

As tensions grew between Romania and the Soviet Union in the 1960s, Moldavian writers used every opportunity to import books from Bucharest and communicate with intellectuals across the frontier. After the death of a well-known Romanian writer, Moldavians expressed their sense of unity in unmistakable terms.[89] In 1965, Moldavian writers, meeting in their third congress, called on the party and government to allow the use of the Roman alphabet, but the party refused.[90] From the 1970s to the present, the government and party in Moldavia have reacted to the nationalism of Romania by trying again to Russify Moldavian and limit efforts to keep a common standard. Intellectuals are reacting by exaggerating their use of the Bucharest standard even to the point of speaking literary Romanian,[91] which could increase the gap between themselves and the large rural population. With the greater freedom offered by *glasnost* and *perestroika,* Moldavians openly demand and use the Roman alphabet and the exclusion of the Russian language from official domains.

CONCLUSION

In all these cases, language form and language function are an explicit instrument in the pursuit of interest, not merely the by-product of economic and political decisionmaking or of the communication marketplace.   Individual writers and linguists have consciously chosen forms of language to shape identities and loyalties.   Governments have also taken the initiative by trying to assimilate people through a change in the official language imposed on them.   Choice of form and function promotes or impedes satisfaction of nonlinguistic interests by attempting to change or to maintain international frontiers.   Language is an independent variable.

Elites in Kosovo, Macedonia, and Moldavia felt blocked in the expression of a valued cultural identity and in their access to other desirable values.   It appears that they have been able to convince enough followers to be loyal to linguistic standards that are identified with a well-defined geographical area.   Credible movements maintain identities and articulate political goals.   Governments of kin states have signaled their support of these efforts, albeit discreetly in the case of Albania and Romania.   Secession accompanied by irredentism seems to be the purpose.   Barring irredentist claims by Bulgaria is the goal in Macedonia, and it is true that other groups within Yugoslavia question, from time to time, the separate status of the Macedonians.   France and Germany alternately imposed their standard languages on Alsace in order to prevent challenge to frontiers established after retrieval of their kin.

In the face of a determined effort of one powerful state to retrieve the people and territory of its weaker neighbors, language planning is no barrier.   In the face of a resolution of one powerful state to hold onto the people and territory claimed by a neighboring state, language planning is no aid to frontier change, at least in the short run.   Over the long term, however, people's opinion of a government and their identification with the country, language, and values it represents do count.   Language planning plays its role in shaping the self-perceptions of large groups of people and in legitimizing or delegitimizing political frontiers.   An alliance of cultural and political elites weds that perception and sense of legitimacy to political goals of independence or to secession and irredentism.

Of all these examples, Macedonia seems to have built the most effective barrier to irredentism, but clearly the Yugoslav state also has much at stake in protecting this republic.   Kosovo elites appear to be creating an effective weapon for secession linked with irredentism.   Alsace seems to be firmly part of France, and language planning activity disturbs Communist party tranquility in Moldavia as it now does in Latvia, Lithuania, and Estonia. What is most interesting is that, despite the overwhelming imbalance in power between language planners and writers on the one hand and the state on the other, cultural elites who plan and write are feared and courted. Under the proper circumstances, a dictionary makes the powerful tremble.

NOTES

1. Donald L. Horowitz, *Ethnic Groups in Conflict* (Berkeley: University of California Press, 1985), p. 282.
2. Brian Weinstein, *The Civic Tongue: Political Consequences of Language Choices* (New York: Longman, 1983), pp. 62–78.
3. Cited in Brian Weinstein, "Noah Webster and the Diffusion of Linguistic Innovations for Political Purposes," *International Journal of the Sociology of Language* 38 (1982): 85–108.
4. Etiemble, as cited in Philippe de Saint Robert, *Lettre ouverte à ceux qui en perdent leur français* (Paris: Albin Michel, 1986), p. 38.
5. Richard E. Wood, "Language Maintenance and External Support: The Case of the French Flemings," *International Journal of the Sociology of Languages* 25 (1980): 107–120, at p. 113.
6. Cited in Roland Willemyns, "Le traité de l'Union de la Langue Néerlandaise," *La Linguistique* 1, 20 (1984): 81–96, at p. 88
7. Ibid., p. 89.
8. Peter R. Prifti, *Socialist Albania since 1944: Domestic and Foreign Developments* (Cambridge, Mass.: MIT Press, 1978), p. 222.
9. Ibid., p. 223.
10. Ibid., p. 225.
11. Ivo Blanc, *The National Question in Yugoslavia: Origins, History, Politics* (Ithaca, N. Y.: Cornell University Press, 1984), p. 298.
12. Ramadan Marmullaku, *Albania and the Albanians* (London: C. Hurst, 1975), p. 140.
13. Cited in Prifti, *Socialist Albania*, p. 228.
14. Cited in Marmullaku, *Albania and the Albanians*, p. 143.
15. Ibid.
16. Ibid., p. 145.
17. Prifti, *Socialist Albania*, p. 229.
18. Marmullaku, *Albania and the Albanians*, p. 150.
19. Pedro Ramet, *Nationalism and Federalism in Yugoslavia 1963–1983* (Bloomington: Indiana University Press, 1984), p. 161.
20. Ibid., p. 164.
21. *Le Monde*, April 9, 1986, p. 6.
22. Nicholaos Stavrou, "Albania," in Richard F. Starr, ed., *1986 Yearbook on International Communist Affairs* (Stanford, Calif.: Hoover Institution Press, 1986), p. 264.
23. Nicholaos Stavrou, personal communication.
24. Nikolaos A. Stavrou, "Origins of the Albanian Communist Movement," *Hellenic Review of International Relations* 3,4 (1983–1984): 73–113, at p. 91.
25. The Albanian Telegraphic Agency (ATA), Tirana, as cited in Stavrou, "Albania," p. 264.
26. Philip Baldi, *An Introduction to the Indo-European Languages* (Carbondale: Southern Illinois University Press, 1983).

27. Stavro Skendi, *The Albanian National Awakening 1878–1912* (Princeton, N. J.: Princeton University Press, 1967), pp. 368–369.

28. Ibid., pp. 370–371.

29. Ibid., p. 376.

30. Ibid., p. 371.

31. Ibid., p. 372.

32. Ibid., p. 381.

33. Blanc, *The National Question in Yugoslavia,* p. 299.

34. Ibid., p. 302.

35. Stavrou, "Origins of the Albanian Communist Movement," p. 75.

36. Blanc, *The National Question in Yugoslavia,* p. 305.

37. Janet Byron, personal communication.

38. Janet Byron, "Language Planning in Albania and in Albanian Speaking Yugoslavia," *Word* 30, 1–2 (April–August 1979): 15–44, at p. 22.

39. Ibid., pp. 32–33.

40. Janet Byron, *Selection Among Alternates in Language Standardization: The Case of Albania* (The Hague: Mouton, 1976), pp. 63, 74–75.

41. Byron, "Language Planning in Albania," pp. 32–33.

42. Ibid., p. 35.

43. Ibid., p. 36.

44. Janet Byron, personal communication, January 17, 1987.

45. Janet Byron, personal communication.

46. Ramet, *Nationalism and Federalism,* p. 166.

47. Ibid., p. 165.

48. Skendi, *The Albanian National Awakening,* p. 14.

49. Marmullaku, *Albania and the Albanians,* p. 88.

50. *New York Times,* July 27, 1986, p. 6.

51. Janet Byron, personal communication.

52. As cited in Walker Connor, *The National Question in Marxist-Leninist Theory and Strategy* (Princeton, N. J.: Princeton University Press, 1984), p. 577, fn. 123.

53. Janet Byron, "An Overview of Language Planning Achievements Among the Albanians of Yugoslavia," *International Journal of the Sociology of Language* 52 (1985): 59–92, at p. 84.

54. Blaže Koneski, "Macedonian," in Alexander M. Schenker and Edward Stankiewicz, eds., *The Slavic Literary Language: Formation and Development* (New Haven, Conn.: Yale Concilium on International and Area Studies, 1980), pp. 53–63, at p. 63.

55. Blaže Koneski, "The Macedonian Dictionary," *Review of National Literatures* 5, 1 (Spring 1974): 25–36, at pp. 33–34.

56. John D. Bell, "Bulgaria," in Richard F. Staar, ed., *1986 Yearbook on International Communist Affairs* (Stanford, Calif.: Hoover Institution Press, 1986), p. 273.

57. Ferdinand Brunot, *Histoire de la langue française des origines à 1900, Tome V, Le français en France at hors de France au XXII siècle* (Paris: Armand Colin, 1927), p. 105.

58. Eugène Philipps, *Les luttes linguistiques en Alsace jusqu'en 1945* (Strasbourg: Culture Alsacienne, 1975), pp. 24–27.

59. Brunot, *Histoire de la langue françasie,* p. 95.

60. Ibid., pp. 104–105.

61. Philipps, *Les luttes linguistiques,* pp. 66–67.

62. See Chapter 3.

63. Philipps, *Les luttes linguistiques,* p. 107.

64. Ibid., p. 131.

65. Ibid., p. 347, fn. 203.

66. See ibid., pp. 189–216, for facts in this paragraph.

67. Ibid., p. 232.

68. Penelope Gardner-Chloros, "Hans im Schnockeloch: Language in Alsace," *Modern Languages* 44, 1 (March 1983): 35–41, at p. 38.

69. This fact, generally known, was taken from Nicholas Dima, *Bessarabia and Bukovina: The Soviet-Romanian Territorial Dispute* (Boulder, Colo.: East European Monographs, distributed by Columbia University Press, 1982), pp. 2–17.

70. Ibid., p. 17.

71. Michael Bruchis, *One Step Back, Two Steps Forward: On the Language Policy of the Communist Party of the Soviet Union in the National Republics (Moldavian: A Look Back, a Survey, and Perspectives, 1924–1980)* (Boulder, Colo.: East European Monographs, distributed by Columbia University Press, 1982), pp. 46–52.

72. Ibid., p. 67.

73. As cited in Connor, *The National Question*, p. 577, fn. 124.

74. Dima, *Bessarabia and Bukovina*, p. 55.

75. Ibid., pp. 58–59.

76. Ibid., p. 127.

77. Robert A. Hall, Jr., *External History of the Romance Languages* (New York, London, Amsterdam: American Elsevier, 1974), pp. 91–92.

78. Ibid., p. 125.

79. Ibid., p. 211, fn. 27.

80. Ibid., p. 201.

81. Dima, *Bessarabia and Bukovina*, p. 48.

82. Barbara A. Anderson and Brian D. Silver, "Equality, Efficiency, and Politics in Soviet Bilingual Education Policy, 1934–1980," *The American Political Science Review* 78 (1984): 1019–1039, at p. 1034.

83. Dima, *Bessarabia and Bukovina*, p. 107.

84. Bruchis, *One Step Back, Two Steps Forward*, p. 83.

85. Ibid., pp. 105–106.

86. Ibid., p. 141.

87. Ibid., p. 110.

88. Ibid., p. 256.

89. Ibid., p. 185.

90. Ibid., p. 289.

91. Dima, *Bessarabia and Bukovina*, p. 99.

Irredentism, Separatism, and Nationalism

NAOMI CHAZAN

Irredentism has been examined in this book from a variety of historical, comparative, disciplinary, and theoretical perspectives. Despite the range of cases presented and the seeming disparity of analytic foci, the contributions included in this volume shed considerable light on the complex relationships among people, states, and territory, which are at the core of the irredentist phenomenon. This concluding chapter seeks to bring together some of the main insights contained in the previous chapters. It focuses on the development of irredentism conceptually, historically, and dynamically and offers some directions for further contemplation and study.

The need to explore the intricacies of the issues surrounding irredentism is particularly urgent today, as the global order, once again, is undergoing profound processes of readjustment that, as the 1990 Gulf crisis demonstrates, inevitably raise essential questions about the criteria for the demarcation of the boundaries of political units and the principles guiding their interaction. The elucidation of the options and difficulties inherent in the redefinition of the bases and frameworks of self-determination in the contemporary world assists in informing choices and delineating alternatives in a climate of uncertainty and change.

THE DEVELOPMENT OF IRREDENTIST CONCEPTS

Irredentism, in broad strokes, refers to attempts by existing states to annex adjacent lands and the people who inhabit them in the name of historical, cultural, religious, linguistic, or geographic affinity. Intrinsic to the notion of irredentism is a tension between people and territory, between politics and culture—indeed, between symbolic and instrumental aspects of international relations.

The contributors to this volume differ among themselves on the relative stress they place on each of these facets in their analyses of irredentism. Donald Horowitz, in Chapter 1, highlights the centrality of people in the irredentist quest: "Irredentism is a movement by members of an ethnic group in one state to retrieve ethnically kindred people and their territory across borders." This emphasis is echoed in Chapter 4 by Reichman and Golan, who reverse the direction of causation by suggesting that irredentism "is a particular facet of nationalism, where a national movement that is a minority in a given territory seeks to rejoin the mother country." Jacob Landau takes this line of thought one step further in Chapter 6 by offering a view of irredentism that stresses "extreme expressions, ideological or organizational, aiming at joining or uniting (i.e., annexing) territories that the ethnic or cultural minority group inhabits or has inhabited at some historical date." He sees irredentism as the outgrowth of "an ideological or organizational expression of passionate interest in the well-being of an ethnic or cultural minority living outside the boundaries of the states inhabited by the same group." In all these definitions not only are subjective, cultural, and symbolic aspects accentuated, but the concept of irredentism is broadened to include possible cases of the creation of new states composed of ethnically or historically related peoples (such as a potential Kurdish, Pan-Arab, or Armenian entity), as well as more standard instances of state expansion under a putative nationalist guise.

Benyamin Neuberger, in contrast, does not entertain such eventualities. In his conceptualization (Chapter 7), irredentism can be understood only if the role of the state—and, by extension, of its instrumental and political concerns—is recognized. In his view, "we must make clear that irredentism means an attempt made by an existing state to 'redeem' territories and peoples it considers its own." This position is accepted in Chapter 8 by Brian Weinstein, who quotes previous work by Donald Horowitz that underscores the role of the state in irredentist processes: "Irredentism may be defined as a 'decision to retrieve group members across a territorial border by forcibly altering the border [and] is a governmental decision.'"[1]

In Chapter 2, Hedva Ben-Israel aptly summarizes the difficulties of grasping the concept of irredentism when she states: "The key aspect of irredentism . . . is the tension between land and people." She opts, however, for a state-oriented perspective: "Irredentism is not just any claim for annexing territory or even adjacent territory with a kin population in it, although this is sometimes the case. Irredentism pertains in the first place to territory demanded by a state on the ground that it had been or should have been an integral part of the national heritage. Ethnic populations often come into it, but it is . . . territory more than population that is central in irredentist movements."

The divergent approaches to the conceptualization of irredentism evident in the chapters in this volume stem from differences in the weight accorded to empirical as opposed to conceptual considerations. Those authors who attribute primary importance to the role of the state in the definition of irredentism base their analyses on actual historical cases, whereas those who favor a broader, culturally oriented definition rely more heavily on hypothetical possibilities which have not necessarily been realized to date.   In either case, these views assist in sharpening and highlighting the territorial element of the irredentist equation and its connection to the states and peoples it encompasses.

The irredentist *phenomenon*, as depicted in these chapters, therefore refers to nationalistically rationalized state territorial expansion. Unlike other types of conquest, irredentism is directed at neighboring countries and contains strong emotional, normative, and subjective dimensions. The irredentist *justification*, therefore, is cultural and symbolic, even when its purpose may be brazenly opportunistic. It is the combination of power and economic considerations (frequently manifest in military terms) coupled with patriotic sentiments and particularistic ideological language that endows irredentism with its unique flavor as the political connecting link between state expansion and nationalist fervor.   Irredentist *processes* refer to the purposeful quest by states to acquire or retrieve territories in the name of the nation they seek to represent, and by definition they possess an international dimension.

The refinement of the definition of irredentist processes and their characteristic features assists in distinguishing irredentism from other related phenomena. As Donald Horowitz emphasizes in his theoretical contribution, irredentism is allied to, but separate from, secession in that it "involves subtracting from one state and adding to another state . . . secession involves subtracting alone." The state, consequently, is essential to irredentist initiatives. Similarly, irredentism differs from ethnicity in that, although frequently evoking symbolic identities of an ethnic sort, it also relies on other rationalizations and focuses squarely on concrete territorial achievements. Irredentism, although often rooted in ethnic geography (which helps to separate irredentism from pan-cultural movements, which may not have precise territorial expressions),[2] does not derive exclusively, if at all, from ethnic considerations. On the other hand, irredentist conflicts are not merely boundary disputes—they do rest heavily on emotional appeals to national sentiments on both sides of international frontiers. Thus, although irredentism is conceptually distinct from ethnicity, separatism, pan-cultural movements, and border skirmishes, it is in fact best characterized as an active mixture of all of these ingredients.

The problematics ingrained in the conceptual development of the notion of irredentism as explored in this volume raise some important questions for future research. First, how can the separate features of each of the concepts related to irredentism—the state, the nation, political boundaries—be further identified and distinguished from each other? Second, when and why does irredentism relate to and interact with ethnicity, nationalism, state organization, cultural proliferation, and territorial expansion? And finally, what tools can be honed to help in further investigating the connections between subjective identities and objective pursuits in the interaction between adjoining states? Answers to these and other related queries can contribute much in illuminating the nature and direction of regional conflicts in the last decade of the present century.

THE DIFFUSION OF IRREDENTIST PROCESSES

Irredentism first emerged as a distinct process in nineteenth-century Europe, when issues of state formation and national awakening converged over the delineation of political boundaries. The historic emergence of irredentism in this setting is crucial. As Hedva Ben-Israel points out: "Modern irredentism is an outcome of the acceptance of the principle of nationalism, that is, the state in which ethnic, cultural, and political boundaries coincide. . . . The principle of the modern nation-state provided the age-long phenomenon of irredentism with its modern rationale and mode of self-expression." The molding of sovereign states defined by national movements clearly furnished the impetus for the geographic diffusion of irredentism during the past century.

The progression of irredentist processes, as described in these pages, occurred in four distinct waves. The first, described by Gutmann and Weinstein but referred to by other authors as well, centered on the delineation of the boundaries of core European states (especially Italy and Germany) during the latter part of the nineteenth and the beginning of the twentieth century.[3] The second phase of irredentist proliferation took place in the interwar years and was largely associated with the redrawing of boundaries after the collapse of the Austro-Hungarian and Ottoman empires and the defeat of greater Germany in World War I. The adoption of the Wilsonian principles of self-determination in the Balkans, and the political decision to bolster the standing of independent Poland, inevitably led to efforts by new states to adjust or consolidate their boundaries by invoking irredentist claims. Reichman and Golan discuss the Polish, Balkan, and Macedonian instances of irredentism during this period, and Ben-Israel skillfully analyzes the Czechoslovak case.

The third wave of irredentism was integrally tied to postwar processes of decolonization. Irredentist-related conflagrations were recorded along the India-Pakistan-Afghanistan boundaries, and in the Middle East on the frontiers of Iran, Iraq, the Soviet Union, Syria, Lebanon, and Turkey. Since the 1960s, as Neuberger recounts, similar incidents, however sporadic, have surfaced in the Horn of Africa, in the Sahara, and in Southern Africa. A fourth, contemporary wave of irredentism has surfaced in the latter part of the twentieth century, once again most emphatically in Europe (with the breakdown of the Soviet bloc) and in the more conflict-prone areas of the Middle East (especially the Persian Gulf), Asia, and Africa.

The timing of the successive phases of irredentist manifestations reveals some of the factors at work in the emergence of these processes. In the first place, irredentist tendencies have inevitably been associated with periods of major political reordering, boundary readjustment, or restructuring of the international system (during the latter part of the nineteenth century, following each of the two world wars, and in the last decade of this century). Second, the appearance of irredentism has often, although by no means exclusively, been linked to periods of war or major conflict (and has often surfaced as a violent outcome of these confrontations). Third, irredentist impulses have usually been tied to the breakdown of empires (the Austro-Hungarian and Ottoman empires, the colonial orders, and the Soviet bloc) and to the quest to establish or assert specific criteria for the demarcation of successor political entities. Fourth, therefore, irredentism has been a by-product of transition and uncertainty in the international order. Irredentist propensities may lie dormant for years (as Jacob Landau and Emanuel Gutmann demonstrate) and then erupt when interstate arrangements are destabilized. The latent and overt phases of irredentism are therefore closely connected to occurrences in the international arena in general and regional politics in particular.

The conditions for the development of irredentist trends also help to explain the geographic diffusion of the phenomenon. Irredentist processes have spread throughout the world, but they have been much rarer in the Americas than in other portions of the globe. In part, the relative absence of irredentism in North and South America may be attributed to the containment of large-scale warfare in these regions. In part, it may be an outgrowth of the relative stability of the continental order. And to no mean extent, the quiescence of irredentist phenomena in the Americas may be due to the fact that in these areas preexisting historical or ethnic units were virtually obliterated at the time of the European conquest. Modern states in the Americas have distinctly preceded nations, and therefore, as Ben-Israel points out, emotional appeals in the name of the past as an instrument of territorial aggrandizement have not achieved the resonance they have gained elsewhere.

The historical progression and geographic spread of irredentism has thus been accompanied by a refinement of a variety of irredentist forms and expressions. Following on Neuberger's classification, it is possible to distinguish various types of redeeming states, ranging from nation-states (Somalia, Italy, Iraq, Germany), quasi nation-states (France, Poland, Togo), historic states (Macedonia, Ethiopia) to plural states (Cameroon, India). There are also multiple definitions of the territories to be redeemed, on the basis of ethnicity, immediate or more remote history, language, and geography. These forms of irredentism reflect the elaboration of statist, ethnocultural, historical, and pluralist notions of self-determination.[4]

Patterns of irredentist dissemination, as depicted in the preceding chapters, follow empirically in the wake of wars and chronologically on successive notions of statism and self-determination.[5] Processes of irredentism coincide with periods of political redefinition, insecurity, introspection, and statist bravado. They have constituted a form of localized regional conflict characterized by particularism and a quest for the revival of some sense of historic community. In this respect, according to Ben-Israel, irredentism has epitomized the triumph of communal identity over principles of pluralism and universal human rights. It is the mixture of power and paranoia that has fueled irredentist urges, and the combination of transition and opportunity that has propelled irredentist claims.

The record of the development and proliferation of irredentism highlights several central issues in the study of the international relations of parochial politics. First, what is the relationship between emotional appeals and ongoing security concerns? Second, when does ethnic contiguity erupt into expansionist claims? Third, under what circumstances do regional tensions assume irredentist markings? And finally, how do shifts in the delineation of the parameters of self-determination occur and how are they subsequently translated into policy terms? Responses to these queries can aid not only in shedding light on heretofore obscure aspects of interstate relations, but also in advancing an understanding of the shifting bases and objectives of self-determination over time.

THE DYNAMICS OF IRREDENTIST MOVEMENTS

If the climate for irredentism is a function of the regional environment, the impetus for irredentist moves lies in domestic political processes. The contributions to this volume trace a variety of irredentist manifestations and painstakingly attempt to account both for the course of irredentist processes and for the paucity of irredentist phenomena.

Irredentist drives, all these authors concur, have always been the conscious culmination of a variety of political, economic, and cultural forces. The recurrence or absence or irredentism is therefore neither random nor haphazard. In general, as Donald Horowitz notes, "There have been remarkably few irredentas . . . but there have been a great many secessionist movements." Thus it is difficult to escape noting the relative infrequency of irredentist processes even when conditions have appeared to favor them.

The rarity of irredentism is attributed, in part, to the attraction of other alternatives. Richard Stoess suggests in Chapter 5 that the appeal of integration in postwar Germany has precluded the rise of major irredentist trends: "Because of the East-West conflict and the iron curtain, which ran through the middle of Germany, there was no realistic alternative to integration into the West." Benyamin Neuberger also underlines the significance of this factor as an impediment to irredentism: "Another reason for the relative absence of ethnic irredenta is the processes of integration that occurred in the colonial and postcolonial periods and that weakened the emotional-ethnic ties to such an extent that the different sections of the partitioned groups developed differential interests, feelings, and identities." And Emanuel Gutmann suggests that regional autonomy or decentralization can avert irredentist predispositions.

Moreover, the convertibility of irredentism and secession has made separatism a much more attractive option, despite its record of failure, especially in the postwar era. Donald Horowitz suggests: "One reason why there are few irredentas may be that many groups that have a choice between irredentism and secession find the latter more satisfying. Indeed, the potential for irredentism may increase the frequency and strength of secession, but not vice versa." Indeed, as Horowitz summarizes: "Underpinning the convertibility of movements is the mutability of ethnic-group claims, of international relations, and of transborder ethnic affinities.   Groups (and states) are not born irredentist or secessionist. They can and do move back and forth from integrated participation in the state of which they are a part to a posture of secession or irredentism."

Irredentist phenomena have been scarce also because they require a very particular combination of political characteristics. First, retrieving states must be strong enough to articulate and press their irredentist claims.   According to Neuberger, soft states—the vast majority of states in the postwar world—have "neither the will nor the capacity to turn 'Jacobin'—to force the partitioned and peripheral groups to assimilate, to conform, or to adapt to the center." Second, utility and perceived interest have always played a role. Because irredentist adventures run the risk of upsetting delicate domestic balances, of splitting public opinion, of being extraordinarily costly, and of ultimately failing, they have not usually been undertaken by government leaders. Third, and not insignificantly, the interests of the leaders of populations to be retrieved do not always encourage irredentism. In fact, many groups that may potentially be the object of irredentist claims do not relish the marginalization that might accompany their "redemption." As Horowitz states, "If claims are convertible from secession to irredenta and vice versa, if transborder affinities are imperfectly developed, if state policy is at best inconstant, and if there is frequently a reluctance to retrieve or be retrieved, the sum of all of this is a powerful structural bias against the incidence of irredentism."

Irredentism, where it does occur, is therefore a product of a behavioral constellation in which instrumental considerations and cultural yearnings overlap. A number of contributors to this volume accentuate the sentimental and subjective features of irredentism. Jacob Landau suggests that "Pan-Turkism is evidently romantic and emotional," and proceeds to state that it has tended to ignore geographic, military, economic, and religious concerns. Hedva Ben-Israel has gone so far as to dub irredentism "the atavistic call of the wild of modern nationalism," which in her mind "recalls the instinctive urge of humans to define their territory in the same way that animals do, although not by the same physical means." But irredentist dynamics are not only symbolic. Irredentism occurs when state leaders adopt and promote parochial ideologies in the name of the national interest (the Iraqi example being a notable case in point). The mechanisms of transitions to irredentist policies do have a logic of their own; it is important to trace their path.

The roots of irredentism lie in the forging of cultural or communal sentiments across state boundaries. The role of cultural elites is crucial in this process. Writers, poets, linguists, and religious leaders have been instrumental in carving out trans-state feelings of identity and in elaborating the means for group communication. Emanuel Gutmann, Jacob Landau, and Richard Stoess highlight the prominence of language carriers in the consolidation of group identities, often as a reaction to intense official efforts to impose cultural homogeneity on diverse populations. Brian Weinstein demonstrates how these leaders have used appeals to language and ethnic affinity to advance their own position: "Nongovernmental cultural elites who initiate language planning are likely to belong to strata of language communities most affected by technological, socioeconomic, and political changes that produce new professions, new classes, and other groups whose interests are not satisfied by existing structures."

The actual inception of irredentist moves has depended heavily on elite interaction. The creation of alliances between cultural and political elites (either domestically or on both sides of international boundaries) has provided the impetus for the dissemination of irredentist notions and set the stage for their translation into policy. As Landau notes: "The propagation of Pan-Turkism in the late Ottoman Empire was largely due, on the one hand, to the activity of Tatar intellectuals who had immigrated from Russia and, on the other hand, to the writings of several Ottoman thinkers. Its penetration of small but influential elitist circles was due in no small degree to the political fortunes and intellectual makeup of the empire."

Several factors have contributed to the consolidation of such irredentist coalitions. The ethnic structure of the country making irredentist claims and of the state against which such claims are made is significant. (When the ethnic group is dominant and in power in the initiating state, it tends to be more receptive to appeals from cultural leaders on both sides of international borders.) So, too, is the degree of intragroup communication on the one hand and intergroup differentiation (frequently on a class basis) on the other. When prospects for group mobility in existing conditions have been limited, the attraction of irredentism grows. Above all, however, the degree to which cultural considerations coincide with the political preferences of governing strata is crucial. At this stage real or perceived pressures on leaders by their constituents, coupled with threats from opposing domestic forces and opportunities offered by regional circumstances, have come into play.

Essentially, the adoption of irredentism as a policy has been, and still is, a purposeful governmental decision arising from elite interlocking (at times coinciding with the rise of new ruling coalitions in the putative irredentist state). According to Weinstein, "language planning plays its role in shaping the self-perceptions of large groups of people and in legitimizing or delegitimizing political frontiers. An alliance of cultural and political elites weds that perception and sense of legitimacy to political goals of independence or to secession and irredentism."

The coincidence of communal ideology and state elite interests is, the contributors to this volume suggest, the crucial turning point in the transition from a nation-state to a communal-state construct.[6] A communal-state is marked not only by an ideology of subjective identification of the common interest with the particularistic symbols and goals of its ethnic majority (and the concomitant abandonment of adherence to universalistic ideological tenets), but also by the commitment of state resources in the pursuit of these objectives at home and abroad.

The pursuit of irredentist objectives therefore magnifies emotional contents but hardly ignores economic, strategic, or security concerns. Irredentist demands have been forwarded, first, in a declaratory manner. Putative irredentist states have laid claim, on the rhetorical level, to their historic right to adjacent territories, and have pronounced their intention of recovering what they perceive to be their national heritage. The escalation of irredentism has usually been accompanied by diplomatic moves aimed at garnering external support (especially after the world wars when boundary adjustments were on the international agenda), by the extension of overt assistance to irredentist movements across borders, by border skirmishes, and in extreme cases by outright declarations of war (the German invasion of the Sudetenland, the Moroccan expansion into the Western Sahara, the Iraqi invasion of Kuwait, and the Somali incursion into the Ogaden, for example). In many instances, however, irredentist ambitions have been acknowledged and settled before the eruption of large-scale violence.

The treatment of irredentist disputes, as described in these pages, highlights four possible options: rejection (the most common form, which then translates into demands for separatism, regional autonomy, or integration); conquest (by which irredentist ambitions are realized through the use of force); imposition (as in the case of the German invasion of Czechoslovakia); and negotiation (which involves international recognition of the justice, however partial, of irredentist aspirations).

Shalom Reichman and Arnon Golan examine three crucial approaches to the settlement of acknowledged irredentist claims: one, which attempts to readjust boundaries in light of economic and ethnic principles (Germany-Poland in the interwar years); a second, which accedes to irredentist demands in territorial terms and foments counterirredentist claims (Italy-Yugoslavia during this period); and a third, which does not involve the redrawing of boundaries but the transfer of populations (Greece and Turkey after the collapse of the Ottoman Empire). In all these instances, the outcomes of irredentist disputes are a result of either interstate negotiation or international acquiescence to territorial acquisition carried out in the name of the irredentist prerogative.

The stability of such arrangements, however, has depended less on international assurances than on social, economic, and cultural processes within specific countries.[7] These findings reinforce the conclusions of many of the contributors to this volume that although the conditions for the emergence of irredentist manifestations are a function of regional and international conjunctures, the mechanisms of the rise, pursuit, and disposition of irredentist procedures (as well as the sustainment of irredentist sentiments) are a product of domestic policies and processes within adjoining states.

The dynamic progression of irredentist movements as depicted in these pages underlines the centrality of regional conflicts in the derivation of irredentist impulses and of domestic social and political trends in the gestation, presentation, mobilization, and ultimate eruption of irredentist disputes. It also highlights the close association between domestic stability based on adherence to some fundamental concepts of pluralism and respect for minority rights and the suppression of irredentist predispositions. Cultural, linguistic, religious, and civic policies consequently play an important role in encouraging or obviating the prospects of irredentist eruptions. The close association between statism and nationalism inevitably fuels irredentist urges; the separation of state interests from communal sentiments has gone a long way toward reducing these tendencies.[8] The management of irredentist forces, much as the curtailment of intense ethnic demands, is therefore a function of a modicum of equity in the disposition of the benefits of socioeconomic and political change.[9] The policy implications that emerge from these studies thus focus on the centrality of regional accommodation, interstate interaction, and domestic stability in the reduction of extreme irredentist tendencies. These connections require additional elaboration and refinement.

THE RAMIFICATIONS OF IRREDENTIST RESEARCH

The exploration of irredentist phenomena has been complicated by the multidisciplinary nature of such inquiries and by their broad historical and comparative scope. The chapters in this book have not attempted to encompass, either theoretically or empirically, the totality of the irredentist experience. They have, however, sought to pinpoint the major preconditions, mechanisms, features, and results of irredentist processes in order to elucidate key facets of interstate relations and to delve more deeply into the forces that activate and shape their development. The historical and comparative analysis of irredentism has significant conceptual and practical repercussions.

The approach to the study of irredentism employed in this collection has been avowedly eclectic. Individual contributors have combined different levels of analysis—moving from the level of individuals and movements to the level of the state and the international arena—in order to depict how particular types and forms of interactions have advanced or impeded irredentist tendencies. They have also sought to examine irredentism in terms of its connection to nationalism, separatism, statism, and ethnicity. The placement of irredentist processes within this rubric not only helped to sharpen an understanding of irredentist tendencies, but also to distinguish such processes from similar but clearly separate phenomena.

The conceptualization of irredentism as the political culmination of communalism, statism, and expansionism in situations of regional uncertainty and in times of political transition is the result of the simultaneous employment of subjective and objective tools of analysis. Indeed, the study of irredentism requires the conscious merging of perceptual and empirical insights in an effort to trace a combination of cultural, emotional, social, and political processes and to investigate some of the consequences of the convergence of symbolic and instrumental interests.

The utility of such an interactive method is not merely academic. Irredentist impulses have emerged in the past as the unintended consequences of interstate tensions and conflict. They have coalesced in an atmosphere of domestic ambiguity and ideological reexamination. And they have frequently served as the precursors of major reevaluations of the structure of the global order. As the twentieth century draws to a close, many of the circumstances and mechanisms that have historically fueled irredentist aspirations appear, once again, to be surfacing. The breakdown of regional hegemonic arrangements in Eastern Europe, the Far East, Africa, and the Middle East inevitably draws attention to the need to redefine political boundaries, reassess ideological tenets, and reconsider national priorities. In this situation the importance of regional relationships is magnified, the possibility of potential irredentist expressions is intensified, and the necessity of regulating the interaction between contiguous states is accentuated.

Domestic political trends in many parts of the world may also be conducive, albeit not always explicitly, to the development of irredentist orientations. The subjugation of state autonomy to the interests of specific social groups in many countries, coupled with the reduction in state capacities and state authority and the accumulation of military might in the hands of erratic leaders, does not augur well for the preclusion of irredentist propensities in certain conflict-prone regions today.

This volume is offered as an initial contribution to the growing need to systematically confront the issues associated with irredentism. I hope the findings it contains will prompt further research and generate additional explorations of this timely but often neglected phenomenon.

NOTES

1. Donald L. Horowitz, *Ethnic Groups in Conflict* (Berkeley: University of California Press, 1985), p. 282. Horowitz goes on to suggest: "In this respect, it [irredentism] differs from the decision to initiate a secessionist movement, which is an ethnic group decision. Group leaders may agitate for a new boundary that embraces group members not within the present boundary, but the irredentist decision, as a matter of state policy, is not simply the product of group sentiment."

2. See Chapter 2.

3. Emanuel Gutmann insists in Chapter 3 that real irredentism took shape only after the process of German unification.

4. For further details, see Benyamin Neuberger, *National Self-*

Determination in Postcolonial Africa (Boulder, Colo.: Lynne Rienner Publishers, 1986), pp. 19–60.

5. For a broad discussion of the development of different concepts of self-determination, see Dov Ronen, *The Quest for Self-Determination* (New Haven, Conn.: Yale University Press, 1979).

6. This terminology was ironed out in a series of conversations with Baruch Kimmerling, whose assistance is gratefully acknowledged.

7. See Chapter 4.

8. Hedva Ben-Israel highlights this connection in her analysis of Jewish irredentist claims for a Greater Israel (Chapter 2).

9. See Donald Rothchild and Victor A. Olorunsola, "Managing Competing State and Ethnic Claims," in Donald Rothchild and Victor A. Olorunsola, eds., *State Versus Ethnic Claims: African Policy Dilemmas* (Boulder, Colo.: Westview Press, 1983), pp. 1–24.

The Contributors _____

NAOMI CHAZAN heads the Harry S. Truman Institute for the Advancement of Peace at the Hebrew University and chairs its academic committee. Professor Chazan teaches political science and African studies at the Hebrew University of Jerusalem and was visiting professor of government at Harvard University, where she also held an appointment as the Matina S. Horner Radcliffe Distinguished Visiting Professor. Author and editor of numerous books and articles, among her recent publications are *Politics and Society in Contemporary Africa* (with Robert Mortimer, John Ravenhill, and Donald Rothchild) and *Coping With Africa's Food Crisis* (edited with Timothy Shaw), both published by Lynne Rienner Publishers in 1988.

HEDVA BEN-ISRAEL is professor of modern history at the Hebrew University of Jerusalem and holder of the Aryeh Ben-Eliezer Chair for the Study of National Movements. Professor Ben-Israel is author of *English Historians of the French Revolution* (Cambridge University Press, 1968) and numerous studies of European history in the interwar period.

ARNON GOLAN is a research student in the Department of Geography at the Hebrew University of Jerusalem. His M.A. thesis was "Boundaries, Demarcations and Population Exchange in Europe After the First World War." His recent research deals with the settlement of Jewish people on land abandoned by Arabs during Israel's War of Independence and after.

EMANUEL GUTMANN is professor of political science at the Hebrew University of Jerusalem. He is the author of numerous works on Israeli politics, and is currently working on two books, one on religion and politics in Israel and the other on the role of religion and churches in the politics of western democracies.

DONALD L. HOROWITZ is the Charles S. Murphy Professor of Law and professor of political science at Duke University. His book *Ethnic Groups in Conflict* was published in 1985. *A Democratic South Africa? Constitutional Engineering in a Divided Society* (University of California Press) will appear early in 1991.

JACOB M. LANDAU is professor of political science at the Hebrew University of Jerusalem. He is the author of numerous books and articles on the contemporary Middle East, on Arab nationalism, and on modern Turkish history and politics. His most recent book is *Pan-Islam* (Oxford University Press, 1990).

BENYAMIN NEUBERGER is associate professor in the Department of Middle Eastern and African Studies at Tel Aviv University. He is the author of *Qadhdhafi's Libya and Chad* (1982), *National Self-Determination in Postcolonial Africa* (1986), and *The Origins and Development of Israel's Democracy* (1990).

SHALOM REICHMAN is professor of geography at the Hebrew University of Jerusalem. His research interests are colonization processes (past and present), with an emphasis on public policy; transportation geography, stressing factors affecting travel demands; determination of political boundaries and administrative limits; and geographic processes in Israel in the first years of independence.

RICHARD STOESS is a researcher at the Central Institute for Social Research and lecturer at the Department of Political Science of the Free University of Berlin. His research is principally in political parties and right-wing extremism. Recent books include *Die extreme Rechte in der Bundesrepublik* (1989), *Sozialer Wandel und Einheitsgewerkschaft* (1989), and *Die Republikaner* (1990). *Politics Against Democracy: Right-Wing Extremism in West Germany* is forthcoming in 1991.

BRIAN WEINSTEIN, professor of political science at Howard University, Washington, D.C., has taught and published about language policy and language planning. His books include *The Civic Tongue: The Political Consequences of Language Choices* (1983) and *Language Policy and Political Development* (edited 1990).

Index

About the Book

Irredentism—the attempt by a sovereign state to expand its territories by seeking to retrieve ethnically related populations and the lands they occupy in neighboring countries—is an outgrowth of the complexities inherent in the lack of coincidence of national and state boundaries. *Irredentism and International Politics* represents a pioneering effort to examine the theory, determinants, dynamics, and consequences of this phenomenon.

The authors draw on an array of historical and contemporary case studies from Europe, Africa, and the Middle East to reassess the relationship among nationalism, ethnicity, and state consolidation and to explore, in particular, the implications of that relationship for international politics.